Island Fox Recovery Program

2010 Annual Report

Natural Resource Report NPS/MEDN/NRR—2012/483

Timothy J. Coonan

National Park Service
Channel Islands National Park
1901 Spinnaker Drive
Ventura, California 93001

Angela Guglielmino

National Park Service
Channel Islands National Park
1901 Spinnaker Drive
Ventura, California 93001

January 2012

U.S. Department of the Interior
National Park Service
Natural Resource Stewardship and Science
Fort Collins, Colorado

Please cite this publication as:

Coonan, T. J. and A. Guglielmino. 2012. Island fox recovery program: 2010 annual report. Natural Resource Report NPS/MEDN/NRR—2012/483. National Park Service, Fort Collins, Colorado.

NPS 159/112287, January 2012

Contents

Contents (continued)

Figures

Tables

Executive Summary

In 2010 the National Park Service continued to implement recovery actions for endangered island fox subspecies on San Miguel Island (*Urocyon littoralis littoralis*) and Santa Rosa Island (*Urocyon littoralis santarosae*). A 10-year program of captive breeding and release of both subspecies was completed in 2008. Island foxes had been removed from the wild for captive breeding on San Miguel in 1999, and on Santa Rosa in 2000. During the 10-year captive breeding program, 138 pups were born in captivity, and 155 foxes were released to the wild, beginning in 2003 on Santa Rosa and 2004 on San Miguel. The San Miguel captive breeding facility was closed in 2007, and the Santa Rosa captive facility was closed in 2008 after the final release of captive foxes in November of that year. Excellent reproduction in the wild, exceeding the per capita reproduction in captivity, was the primary reason for ending captive breeding. Also, predation by golden eagles (*Aquila chrysaetos*) had been almost completely mitigated during the 10-year time period, and wild island fox survival rose to 80-90% on both islands.

The park's island fox program has entered an intensive monitoring phase to insure that recovery continues apace, and to eventually document attainment of criteria which would allow delisting of the two subspecies. The excellent survival and reproduction in the wild has allowed rapid growth of the small, recovering populations, and by the end of 2010 the San Miguel island fox population estimate was 315 adults (Fig. 1) and 516 total foxes, numbers which are comparable to population levels prior to the predation-caused decline of the 1990s. In 2010 the Santa Rosa fox population declined, primarily due to predation by golden eagles in spring 2010. The adult population estimate fell from 187 in 2009 to 169 in 2010, and the estimated total number of foxes declined from 389 to 292.

Annual survival of released and wild-born foxes continued to be high on San Miguel (90%) where 7 radiocollared foxes died in 2010, though none from eagle predation. Although annual survival had been above 80% on Santa Rosa in the previous three years, it declined to 66% in 2010 (by March 2011 it had climbed to 79%). Eleven radiocollared foxes died on Santa Rosa in 2010, and 7 of those mortalities were due to predation. Feathers found at one mortality site were identified as golden eagle feathers, and golden eagles were observed on 5 March and 7 March on Santa Rosa Island. A helicopter survey and net-gun effort on 12 March failed to detect any golden eagles on Santa Rosa Island, and no predation-caused mortalities occurred after early April.

Other mortality factors included two cases of possible leptospirosis on Santa Rosa Island. The two mortalities from which *Leptospira* was identified via polymerase chain reaction (PCR) evaluation of tissue, occurred within 50 m of each other but several months apart. Leptospirosis, which causes kidney failure, had not been previously known in island foxes, and is caused by various serovars of the bacterium *Leptospira interrogans*. Antibodies from several serovars had been previously detected in fox blood samples from several islands, but never at high titers. In 2010 we detected high seroprevalence and high titers to *Leptospira* serovars Bratislava and Pomona in island fox blood samples from Santa Rosa Island. The host for the former is mice, while the host for the latter can be skunks or pinnipeds. Because those two serovars can cross-react at high titers, it is

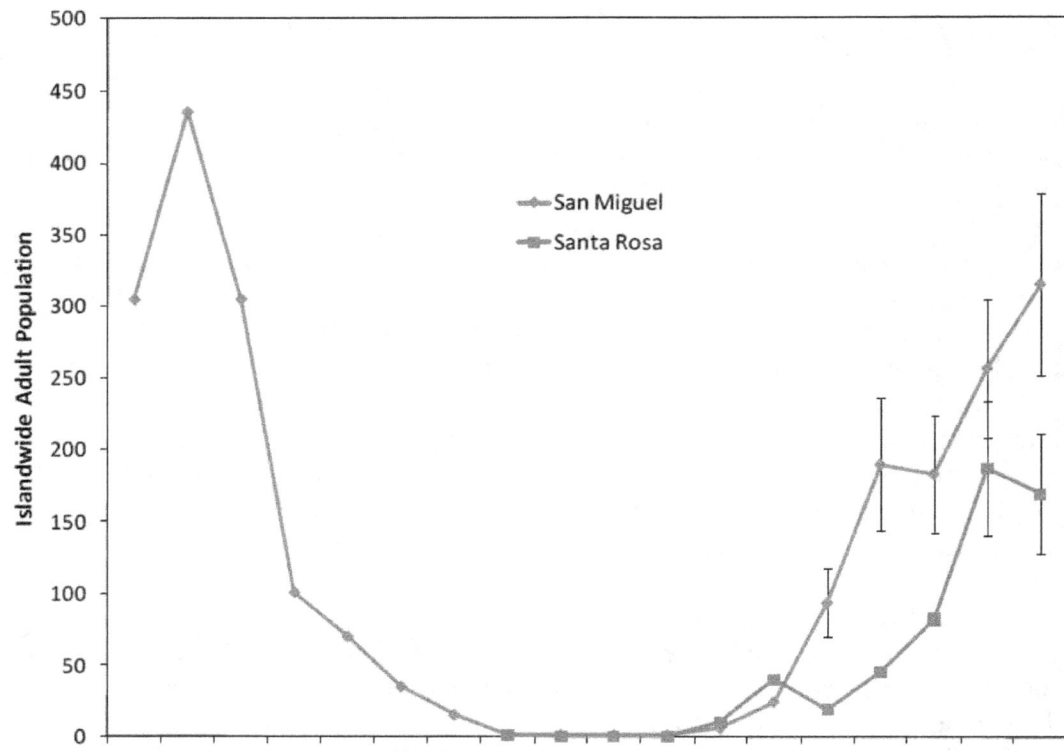

Figure 1. Annual estimated number of adult island foxes for San Miguel and Santa Rosa. Pre-decline estimates are not available for Santa Rosa; 80% confidence intervals are shown for estimates from program Density.

necessary to actually culture the bacteria to determine which serovar is present. Urine samples were obtained from island foxes and island spotted skunks (*Spilogale gracilis amphiala*) in February 2011, and *Leptospira* was successfully cultured from two fox and two skunk samples. By April 2011 the serovar had been preliminarily identified as Pomona. Fox blood samples from San Miguel were negative for Leptospira. The apparent outbreak may be over. Titers declined in several foxes from July to December, though the successful culturing of *Leptospira* from foxes and skunks in February 2011 meant those animals were actively shedding the bacteria.

We conducted grid trapping in summer-fall 2010 to monitor the wild populations on each island. On San Miguel we trapped foxes on 4 small (3 x 6 trap) grids, in order to estimate fox density, replace radiocollars, gauge reproduction through capture of pups, vaccinate wild foxes, and check physical conditions. A total of 79 individuals was trapped on the grids in 2010. The adult density estimates for the 4 grids, as calculated with program Density, were 2.7, 8.8, 11.2 and 10.0 foxes/km^2. Multiplying the average adult density (8.2 foxes/km^2) by the island area (38.1 km^2) yielded a population estimate of 315 adult foxes. When pups were included in density estimates, the total islandwide population was 516 foxes. The average annual rate of increase (lambda) for the San Miguel island fox population for 2004 (when reintroductions began) through 2010 was 1.59.

A total of 32 wild-born pups were caught on the San Miguel grids during fall trapping. Reproductive success was estimated as the number of grid pups divided by the number of adult females caught on the grids (17). The estimated reproductive success of 1.88 pups per female was higher than last year's estimate (0.84), perhaps due to good post-drought resource availability. As expected due to density-dependence, reproductive success has generally declined as the wild fox population has grown.

From 2004-2008, trapping on Santa Rosa was conducted on transects, which precluded estimation of density and islandwide population size. In 2009 we began conducting trapping on 18 small "ladder" grids, as recommended by Rubin et al. (2005). In 2010 average density on the 18 grids was 0.86 foxes/km^2, and multiplying that by the island area (216 km^2) produced an adult density estimate of 169. Including pups in the analysis resulted in an islandwide population estimate of 292 foxes. Both values represented declines from 2009, likely due to higher predation that reduced annual survival. To estimate reproductive effort, we used the number of pups recorded on both the trapping grids and on the transects, which are used to manage radiocollars and vaccinate foxes. The reproductive effort was 0.78 pups/female, which was lower than last year's estimate on Santa Rosa (1.10) and this year's estimate on San Miguel (1.88). The high predation in spring 2010 may have resulted in considerable mortality of breeding females, and thus lower reproductive success.

As in 2009, we were able to estimate the size of the island spotted skunk population on Santa Rosa Island, because we marked individual skunks with passive integrated transponder (PIT) tags. We used program Density on skunk capture data from the 18 ladder grids to obtain a mean skunk density of 13.5 skunks/km^2 and an islandwide estimate of 2,911 skunks. This is comparable to last year's estimate of 3,013 skunks. The estimate includes both adults and juveniles, which were not distinguished from each other in the field. Thus, skunks were almost 8 times as abundant as island foxes. Even so, relative capture rates from 2010 and previous years indicate that skunks are decreasing as the fox population recovers. When foxes were absent from the wild on Santa Rosa, there may have been over 4,000 skunks on the island.

Genetic studies of golden eagles completed in 2010 revealed that island colonization by mainland eagles was likely a one-time event. These results support previous observations that golden eagles removed from the islands will likely not return, especially in the presence of re-established bald eagle populations.

Over 70% of trapped foxes were vaccinated against rabies, and 78% against canine distemper virus. Number of vaccinates for rabies was 97 on San Miguel and 111 on Santa Rosa, while the number of foxes vaccinated against CDV was 114 on each island. We do not encounter and handle enough foxes to follow the 'vaccinated core' strategy, in which 80-100 foxes in one area of the island are vaccinated against CDV (which allows for natural immunity from the endemic strain of CDV in island foxes). We continue to follow the "small population" strategy of vaccinating almost all animals against both diseases.

Acknowledgements

We would like to thank our dedicated island fox crew for gathering the data for this report. Because of their efforts we have excellent information on the status and trend of island fox populations in the park. Island fox staff in 2010 included Jen Savage, Donivan Sphar, Lisa Drake and Jim Howard; they were capably supervised by Helen Fitting.

In 2010 we benefited from the work conducted by a number of volunteers: Dax Brennon, Jenna Duarte, Francesca Ferrara, Mark Huelly, Stephanie Klein, Sarah Lapidus, Dan Olmstead, Lauren Perry, Ivette Plascencia, Megan Richards and Sara Snyder.

We appreciate the support of our partners at the Institute for Wildlife Studies: Dave Garcelon, Brian Hudgens, Pete Sharpe, Don Jones and Kim smith; they are a constant source of assistance and inspiration in our monitoring and conservation efforts. We continue to work closely with our neighbor, The Nature Conservancy, on Santa Cruz Island, and we appreciate our close relationship with Lotus Vermeer and Christie Boser of their staff.

Thanks to Brett West and Yvonne Morales for facilitating purchase of supplies and materials for the fox program. The GPS and proximity collars used on Santa Rosa and San Miguel, respectively, were obtained by Kathy Ralls and Brian Cypher.

We appreciate the continued support of the Island Fox Conservation Working Group, whose support and critical review over the years has focused and improved our recovery efforts.

Island fox recovery at the park would not be possible without the continued support of Kate Faulkner, Russell Galipeau, Dave Graber and Peter Dratch.

Introduction

Background

The island fox, a diminutive relative of the gray fox (*Urocyon cinereoargenteus*), is endemic to the California Channel Islands. The fox is recognized as a different subspecies on each of the 6 largest islands, a distinction upheld by morphological and genetic work (Wayne et al. 1991; Collins 1993). In 2004, the U.S. Fish and Wildlife Service listed as endangered four island fox subspecies, including the three subspecies in Channel Islands National Park (San Miguel Island fox [*U. littoralis littoralis*], Santa Rosa Island fox [*U. l. santarosae*], and Santa Cruz Island fox [*U. l. santacruzae*]), as well as the subspecies on Santa Catalina Island (*U. l. catalinae*) (U.S. Fish and Wildlife Service 2004). The three park subspecies had declined due to high levels of predation by golden eagles (*Aquila chrysaetos*), whereas the Santa Catalina subspecies had declined due to canine distemper virus (CDV; Timm et al. 2009).

Dramatic fox population declines on San Miguel and Santa Cruz Islands were detected during the 1990s. The island fox population on San Miguel declined from an estimated 450 adults in 1994 to 15 in 1999 (Coonan et al. 2005). The Santa Cruz population declined from as many as 2,000 adults in 1994 to 50–60 in 2000 (D. Garcelon, Institute for Wildlife Studies, unpublished data). Foxes on Santa Rosa may have numbered more than 1,500 in 1994 (Roemer et al. 1994) but declined to 15 animals by 2000 (Coonan and Rutz 2001). Prior to implementation of island fox recovery efforts, Roemer (1999) estimated time to extinction at five years for island foxes on San Miguel and 12 years for island foxes on Santa Cruz.

Evidence from radiotelemetry studies showed that predation by golden eagles was the primary mortality factor for island foxes on the northern Channel Islands, and caused the massive decline of the three northern subspecies from 1994 to 2000 (Roemer et al. 2001). Golden eagle predation was identified as the cause of death for 19 of 21 radiocollared island foxes on Santa Cruz Island from 1993 to 1995 (Roemer et al. 2001). On San Miguel Island in 1998–1999, four of eight radio-collared island foxes were killed by golden eagles in a 4-month period (Coonan et al. 2005).

Until the 1990s, golden eagles had never bred on the Channel Islands, and their recent colonization of the islands was due to a prey base, feral pigs (*Sus scrofa*) and mule deer (*Odocoileus hemionus*), that was not present prehistorically (Latta et al. 2005; Collins and Latta 2006). The absence of bald eagles (*Haliaeetus leucocephalus*), which bred historically on the islands and whose presence may have kept golden eagles away, may also have allowed golden eagle colonization of the islands (Roemer et al. 2001). Island foxes evolved in the absence of significant diurnal aerial predators such as golden eagles, and therefore may have been more vulnerable to predation than other small carnivores. Moreover, on much of the northern Channel Islands, historic sheep grazing changed the predominant vegetation from shrub to non-native grasslands, which offer much less cover from aerial predators.

Recovery Actions

Upon receiving recommendations from a convened panel of experts, the Park began taking emergency recovery actions in 1999, focusing on two measures, the removal of the existing golden eagles on the islands, and captive breeding of the critically low island fox populations. In the summer of 1999, the Park constructed pens on San Miguel and began capture of wild island foxes for captive propagation. By January 2000, 14 island foxes had been captured and placed in the pens, leaving only one in the wild. Four of the captured foxes were males and were paired with four females for breeding. In 2004, after five years of breeding, the San Miguel captive population had increased to 50 animals, exceeding the target captive population size of 40 animals and allowing initial releases back to the wild in fall 2004. The San Miguel captive breeding and reintroduction program ended in 2007, due to high reproductive success and survival in the wild. During nine years of captive breeding, 53 pups were born in captivity, and 62 foxes released to the wild. The recovering wild population has steadily increased since releases began in 2004 (Coonan and Schwemm 2009).

A captive breeding program was initiated for Santa Rosa Island in 2000. The initial captive population on Santa Rosa was 15 animals, which proved to be the island's remaining fox population. Some females were pregnant when captured, and three litters were born in captivity in 2000. With an increase to 56 foxes in 2003, the captive population on Santa Rosa exceeded the target captive population size of 40 foxes, and initial releases began in winter 2003/2004. Annual releases continued through 2008, after which captive breeding was ceased on Santa Rosa. In nine years of captive breeding, 87 pups were born in captivity, and 93 foxes (including some of the foxes originally brought into captivity) were released to the wild.

Captive breeding was also conducted on Santa Cruz Island as a joint venture by NPS and The Nature Conservancy, which owns two-thirds of that island. The status of eagles and foxes on Santa Cruz Island was assessed at the 2001 meeting of the Island Fox Conservation Working Group, and consensus was that captive breeding was warranted for that island fox population. In February 2002, a 10-pen captive breeding facility was built on Santa Cruz Island by the National Park Service and The Nature Conservancy. This facility was stocked with 12 adult island foxes caught as known pairs or individuals from separate areas of the island. A second facility was added in 2004. No releases occurred in either 2004 or 2005, and the captive population grew to 62 animals in 2005. Releases occurred from 2006–2007, after which the program ceased due to good reproductive success and breeding in the wild.

The Park established a cooperative agreement with the Santa Cruz Predatory Bird Research Group (SCPBRG) in 1999 for the purpose of relocating golden eagles from the northern Channel Islands. Personnel from the SCPBRG began eagle surveys and removal on Santa Cruz Island, the island with the most recent sightings, in late summer 1999. Golden eagles were discovered breeding on both Santa Cruz and Santa Rosa Islands. By the end of 2006, 44 golden eagles had been removed, mostly from Santa Cruz Island, the majority by bownet trapping. Captured birds were released in northeastern California, and satellite telemetry on the first released birds indicates that none attempted to return to the islands (Latta et al. 2005).

In 2003, the Park completed a recovery strategy for island foxes on the northern Channel Islands (Coonan 2003). The recovery strategy was in the format of a U.S. Fish and Wildlife Service recovery plan, identifying threats to the species, delineating goals, objectives and recovery criteria, and presenting a schedule and cost estimates for recovery actions. Appropriate recovery goals for each of the three island fox subspecies in the northern Channel Islands were determined via demographic modeling (Roemer et al. 2001b). Population viability analysis was used to identify target population levels that would minimize the chance of extinction. Modeling was then used to set an augmentation (captive breeding and release) schedule that would achieve those targeted goals in a reasonable timeframe. The Park's island fox recovery strategy will be superseded by an official island fox recovery plan currently being developed under the direction and authority of the U.S. Fish and Wildlife Service.

The decade of recovery actions has resulted in notable progress toward island fox recovery (Coonan and Schwemm 2009). Island fox populations on the northern Channel Islands have increased from 15 apiece on San Miguel and Santa Rosa and <80 on Santa Cruz to populations that number in the hundreds on the former islands and close to 1,000 on Santa Cruz. This is due to the success of captive breeding and reintroduction, and the success of golden eagle removal. Reintroduced foxes and their progeny reproduced readily in the wild, and survival increased to over 90% on all three islands as golden eagle presence and predation decreased. Rapid population growth has moved each population toward levels that indicate recovery and likelihood of persistence over time (Bakker and Doak 2009). The large-scale ecosystem restoration actions of feral pig removal and bald eagle reintroduction have nudged the islands' ecosystem toward a point which favors fox persistence and discourages future golden eagle colonization of the islands. The court-ordered removal of non-native mule deer (*Odocoileus hemionus*) and elk (*Cervus elephus*) from Santa Rosa Island in 2011 will remove the last of the non-native prey base from the northern Channel Islands.

Ecological Effects of Changes in Fox Abundance
Island fox decline and recovery has caused changes in the islands' ecosystem structure and function, some of which can be tracked via both annual island fox population monitoring and the park's long-term ecological monitoring program (see Ch. 14, The Ecological Role of Island Foxes, in Coonan et al. 2010). Recorded changes due to the absence – and reappearance – of island foxes include those in deer mouse (*Peromyscus maniculatus*) and landbird populations. In addition, island spotted skunks (*Spilogale gracilis amphiala*) are the only other terrestrial carnivores on the Channel Islands, and inhabit Santa Cruz and Santa Rosa Islands. Island spotted skunks compete with island foxes, and increased when foxes declined on both islands in the mid-1990s (Crooks and Van Vuren 2002). As foxes recover, island spotted skunks may decrease, and this interaction may be tracked via island fox population monitoring.

Integrated Island Fox Recovery Team

From 1999–2003, the NPS annually convened a group of experts to help evaluate the status of island foxes on Park lands, and to make findings regarding appropriate recovery actions. The Island Fox Conservation Working Group (IFCWG) comprised a loose affiliation of public agency representatives, landowners, conservancies, zoological institutions, non-profits, and academics concerned about conservation efforts for the island fox. The working group served as a forum for information exchange and evaluation of recovery efforts, dividing into subject matter groups to tackle most issues. The group annually reported the status of island foxes on all islands and listed findings in regard to threats to the species and appropriate mitigation actions (see Appendix A in Coonan et al. 2004).

After listing four island fox subspecies as endangered in 2004, the U.S. Fish and Wildlife Service established an island fox recovery team that retained the characteristics of the IFCWG. Although many recovery teams comprise a small number of individual experts, the Service established an integrated island fox recovery team comprising all 70+ individuals from the former working group. The individuals served as members of specific technical expertise groups, from which individuals were chosen to work on task forces in response to requests from land management agencies (NPS, TNC, Catalina Island Conservancy) regarding management and recovery of island foxes. The task requests were allocated to task groups by the island fox recovery coordination group, which also received the resulting analyses from the task groups and passed on recommendations to the land management agencies, via the Service.

The integrated island fox recovery group first met in June 2004 to establish technical expertise groups and task forces, and begin addressing the task requests formulated by the land management agencies. The team met again in 2005 and 2006 to exchange information on fox conservation and research, review completed work on task requests and recommendations to land managers, continue work on task requests, and provide input to FWS on development of the draft island fox recovery plan (which had been tasked to the recovery coordination group). The 2007 island fox meeting marked a return to a format similar to the island fox conservation working group meetings. This included exchange of information and small workgroups addressing issues raised by the land management agencies, but not in the formal task analysis request process established by FWS.

A smaller group, the Recovery Coordination Group, was tasked by the U.S. Fish and Wildlife Service with developing an island fox recovery plan, and the annual island fox meetings in 2005 and 2006 were used to develop recovery actions, criteria and strategies for inclusion in the plan. As of 2010 the plan had not been released to the public, but the process of developing island fox recovery criteria based on demographic modeling had been published (Bakker and Doak 2009). Information on the integrated island fox recovery team, and on the draft island fox recovery plan, is available from the Ventura Field Office of the U.S Fish and Wildlife Service.

Island Foxes and Long-term Ecological Monitoring

Island foxes have been monitored at Channel Islands National Park since 1993, when annual population monitoring of San Miguel Island foxes was begun as a result of the Park being designated as a Prototype Park for the NPS Inventory and Monitoring Program (Davis et al. 1994). The park was one of a handful at which such comprehensive ecological monitoring was initiated. Island foxes were chosen to monitor because the species was the largest native terrestrial vertebrate on the islands, was endemic to them, and existed at population sizes small enough to render them vulnerable to disease or stochastic demographic declines. The decision to monitor island foxes proved prescient when the monitoring program detected the predation-caused massive decline of San Miguel Island foxes in the mid to late 1990s (Coonan et al. 1998, 2005b).

The early population monitoring, now considered a legacy monitoring protocol, utilized large (7 x 7) grids to estimate island fox density (Fellers et al. 1988, Roemer et al. 1994). That monitoring ended in 1999, when the remaining foxes on San Miguel (15 individuals) were brought into captivity. Current island fox monitoring methods were borne of the 10-year island fox recovery effort (Coonan et al. 2010), in addition to the basic monitoring conducted through the I&M Program. These methods, which have been used since foxes were first reintroduced to the wild in 2003/2004, utilize smaller grids to estimate density, and couple that with mortality monitoring via radiotelemetry (Coonan et al. 2005a). The latter began in 1998, during the final stages of the decline, and was used to identity golden eagle predation as the cause of the decline. Mortality monitoring and annual density estimation are currently viewed as appropriate, and even necessary, for tracking island fox recovery and for detecting future threats to island foxes (Rubin et al. 2007), and are being implemented on all six islands where foxes exist. The park's current methods for monitoring foxes will be described in detail and subjected to peer-review in an NPS island fox monitoring protocol to be published through the Mediterranean Coast Network of the NPS I&M Program.

This report covers island fox recovery actions conducted by park staff in calendar year 2010. The recovery actions, which included island fox population and mortality monitoring, were conducted under U.S. Fish and Wildlife Service Recovery Permit TE86267-0, which has separate reporting requirements (Coonan 2011). Island foxes have been monitored since reintroductions began in 2003. Prior to the catastrophic decline of the 1990s, island fox population monitoring was conducted on San Miguel Island as part of the park's longterm ecological monitoring program (Coonan et al. 1998).

This report presents the results of our efforts in 2010 to capture and monitor island fox populations on San Miguel and Santa Rosa Island via small trapping grids and transects, and to track annual survival and mortality causes via radiotelemetry. The purpose of the monitoring was to:

- assess condition of individual foxes
- replace radiocollars or affix new radiocollars as required
- establish a "sentinel" group of unvaccinated, radiocollared animals
- vaccinate foxes against canine distemper virus and rabies
- estimate density and islandwide population size

Methods

Population Monitoring of Wild Foxes

On San Miguel, grid trapping for density estimation was conducted from late August to early October, and transect trapping to manage collars, establish sentinels and administer vaccines was conducted from July through December. On Santa Rosa, grid trapping was conducted July - August, and transect trapping from August through December. in both cases box traps (23 by 23 by 66 cm, Tomahawk Live Trap Co., Tomahawk, WI) were baited with dry and wet cat food and a fruit scent (Knob Mountain Raw Fur Co., Berwick, PA). Captured foxes were protected from the elements by careful placement of traps, and by a shadecloth cover on each trap. A polyethlylene tube chew bar was wired inside each trap to reduce incidence of tooth damage. Traps were checked once, in the morning, during every 24-hr period.

Upon first capture, animals were weighed in the trap, and then removed and handled without anesthesia for a complete work-up. Data collected included sex, reproductive status, age class, and general physical condition (e.g., condition of coat, presence of ectoparasites, injuries). Captured foxes were marked with passive integrated transponder (PIT) tags (Biomark, Boise, ID) inserted subcutaneously between and just anterior to the scapulae. Single-use sterile PIT tag applicators were used in order to minimize transfer of pathogens. Prior to insertion of the PIT tag, the insertion site was cleaned and disinfected with alcohol, and antibacterial ointment was applied to the needle.

For foxes which had never been captured before, a blood sample was collected from the femoral or jugular vein of captured foxes, separated into its component fractions by centrifugation, and stored for later genetic and serologic analyses. Up to 10 ml of blood was collected from adult (>1.25 kg) foxes, and up to 5 ml from pups. A portion of the serum from each was set aside for archiving at the Institute for Wildlife Studies. Additionally, a portion of the blood samples collected were to be sent to the American Museum of Natural History, under a recent national agreement between that institution and the NPS for archiving biological specimens of endangered species.

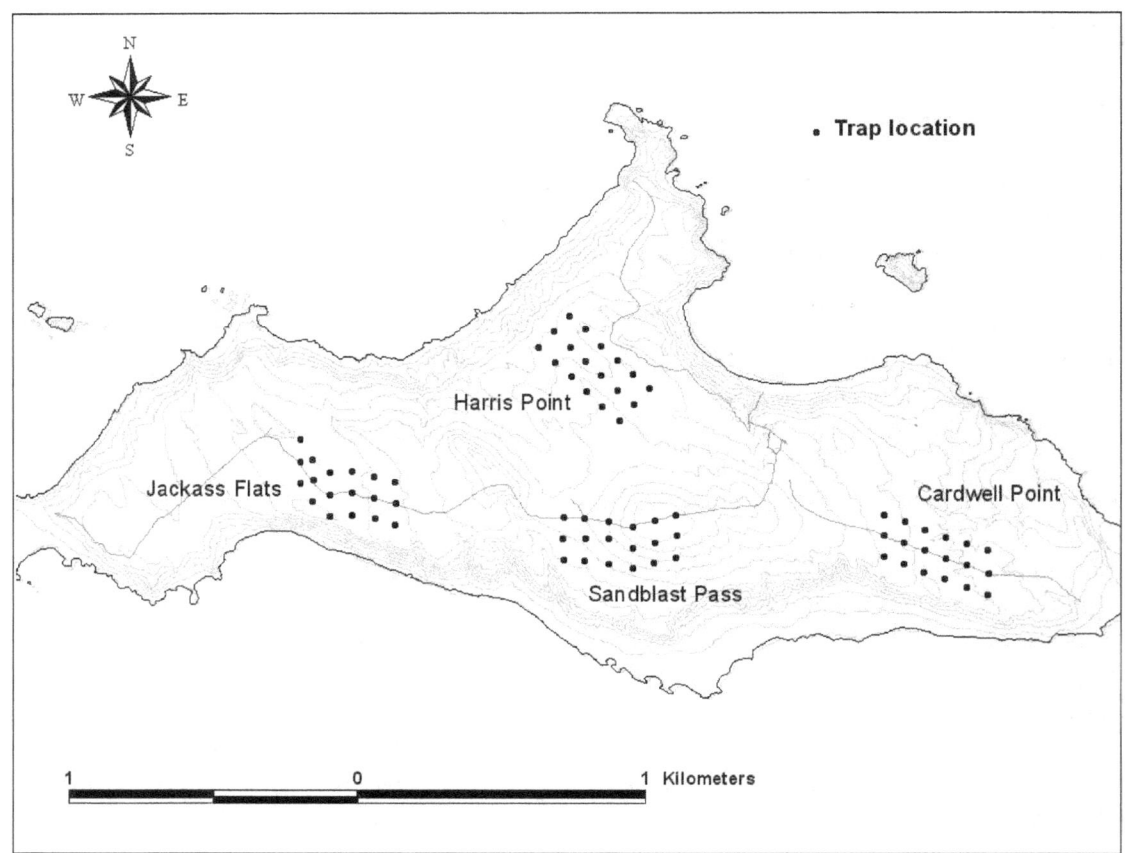

Figure 2. Location of trapping grids, San Miguel Island.

Trapping data was used to estimate distribution and abundance of island foxes, through such measures as trapping success, age structure and sex ratio of foxes, and reproductive success (ratio of number of pups to number of adult females). To estimate density and islandwide population size, 4 small (3 x 6) grids (Fig. 2) were trapped on San Miguel. Three grids were randomly distributed along the primary east-west cross-island trail and a fourth was placed north of the central dunes and south of Hurricane Deck/Harris Point, in the only area without cultural resources. For each grid, one line of traps was dispersed along the trail at 250m intervals, with another line of traps directly north and south of each trap-point on the trail. The grids were designed to be relatively easy to set up and trap, so that a 2-person crew could trap one grid per week while still performing other duties (such as monitoring radiocollared foxes). The grids were run for 5 nights.

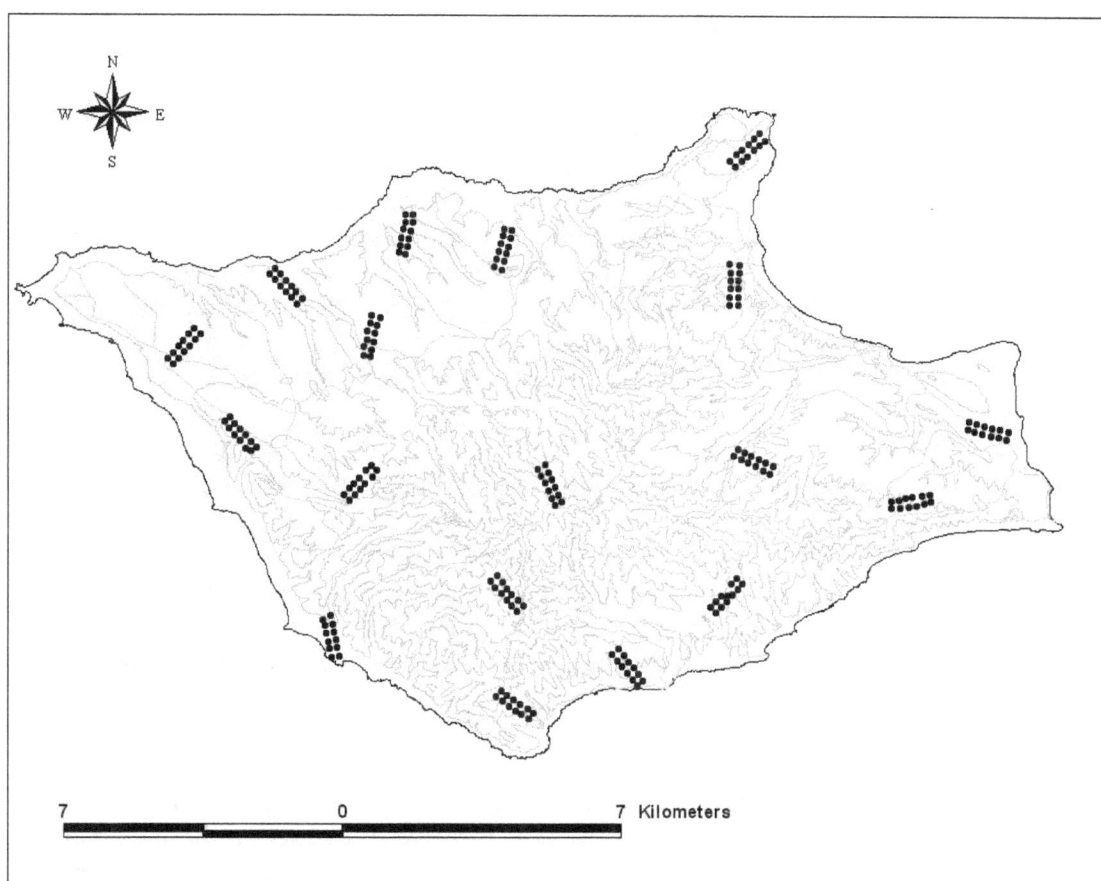

Figure 3. Location of 18 "ladder" grids, Santa Rosa Island.

Previous population monitoring on Santa Rosa utilized line transects, from which it is difficult, if not impossible, to estimate density and thus islandwide population size. Therefore in 2009 we shifted to grid monitoring, and established 18 "ladder" grids (Fig. 3), each comprising a 2 by 6 trap array, as recommended by Rubin et al. (2005). Each grid was run for 6 nights.

Capture-recapture data from each grid was analyzed via program Density (Efford et al. 2004), which models captures as a joint function of density (D), detection (g0), and spatial scale or movement (σ) parameters. We used the maximum likelihood estimator and considered each grid to be a separate trapping session. Average density from the grids was multiplied by island size to estimate island-wide fox population size. Both the standard error for the average density and the standard error for the island-wide population estimate were calculated via the delta method (Cooch and White 2006).

During trapping on Santa Rosa, we also marked island spotted skunks with PIT tags, and so were able to estimate skunk density and islandwide population size.

Survival and Mortality Causes

On both islands, mortality-sensing radio-telemetry collars were placed on a subset of captured foxes in order to assess mortality rates and factors. Collared foxes were monitored regularly to determine their general location and signal type (normal or mortality). If a mortality signal was detected, the dead fox was located and recovered. Data collected at the site prior to removing the carcass included: 1) any information that might indicate cause of mortality, 2) the position of the carcass with respect to its surroundings, including digital photographs, and 3) the general condition of the animal (e.g., eviscerated, intact, damage by insect scavengers, etc.). The location of the carcass was recorded via GPS, and a general description of the habitat was recorded.

Carcasses were tagged with pertinent identification, date and location information. If carcasses could be brought to the mainland within 48 hours of being located, they were refrigerated; otherwise they were frozen and then shipped by overnight carrier to the California Animal Health & Food Safety Laboratory System in Davis, California (Leslie Woods, DVM) for necropsy. Because freezing of tissues increases autolysis, and therefore decreases data that can be extracted from histological examinations, it is advantageous to have the animal necropsied as soon as possible after death and to avoid freezing if possible. If disease was suspected in the death of the animal, tissues were prepared for histological analysis.

Annual survival of radiocollared foxes was estimated with the non-parametric Kaplan-Meier procedure with staggered entry of foxes as they were released to the wild, and of wild-born foxes as they were radio-collared (Pollock et al. 1989). We calculated an 80% confidence interval about the annual survival rate, as the 95% confidence interval is too conservative (V. Bakker, University of California, Davis, and D. Doak, University of Wyoming, pers. comm.).

For both subspecies we used the islandwide population estimate and annual mortality (1 − annual survival) to determine if the recovering fox population met draft demographic recovery criteria being developed by the U.S Fish and Wildlife Service for its island fox recovery plan. Recent demographic modeling incorporated life-history characteristics of the well-studied island fox with environmental drivers and uncertainty to develop extinction probabilities for combinations of population size and annual mortality (Bakker et al. 2009). We plotted 3-year averages of adult population size and adult annual mortality to determine if those values resulted in acceptable extinction risk (5% over 50 years). We used a spreadsheet tool developed by Vicki Bakker of the University of Arizona. The tool plots current values against isoclines representing various levels of extinction risk for island foxes on each island (Bakker and Doak 2009).

Vaccination of Wild Foxes and Establishment of Sentinel Animals

A subset of captured foxes was vaccinated against canine distemper virus and rabies. Although vaccination of wild animals in national parks is rare, vaccination is the best strategy for mitigating possible outbreaks of CDV and rabies in island foxes, because a decline would not be detected quickly enough through monitoring of radiocollared foxes (see below). Consequently, the IFCWG has recommended that 80-100 foxes on each island be vaccinated against CDV, and all captured foxes should be vaccinated against rabies (see Appendix A in Coonan 2010). Not all foxes are vaccinated against CDV in order to protect the naturally-occurring CDV-like morbillivirus that circulates in island fox populations and provides some immunity (Clifford et al. 2006). Selected animals were vaccinated with Purevax Ferrett Distemper Vaccine for CDV and Imrab 3 for rabies (Merial, Inc., Atlanta, GA).

In 2010 we continued to establish a sample of radiocollared sentinel animals on each island. In order to detect disease outbreaks (other than CDV or rabies) the IFCWG has recommended that each island have up to 20 juvenile (1-2 year old) foxes that are unvaccinated (see Appendix A in Coonan 2010). As our wild populations on San Miguel and Santa Rosa have grown, it has become possible to establish sentinels on both islands. During trapping season in 2010 we affixed radiocollars to a number of unvaccinated juvenile foxes for this purpose.

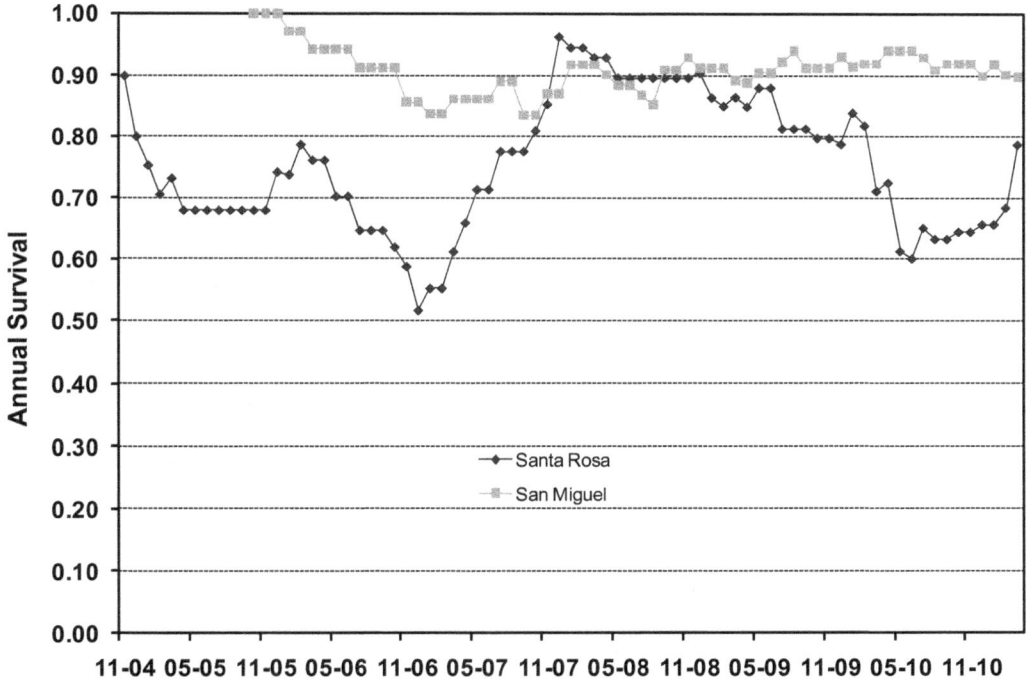

Figure 4. Rolling annual Kaplan-Meier survival for island foxes, San Miguel and Santa Rosa islands.

11

Results and Discussion

San Miguel Island

Mortality Monitoring

Throughout 2010 we maintained a sample of 52-62 radiocollared foxes on San Miguel, and by the end of the year there were 57 radiocollared foxes being monitored. Collared foxes included those previously released from captivity and some wild-born foxes. Annual survival for San Miguel island foxes in 2010 was 90.0% (80% CI = 86-95%). Annual survival has remained above 80% since foxes were first released on San Miguel in 2004 (Fig. 4).

Six radiocollared foxes died in 2010, none from eagle predation (Table 1). Most mortalities were of older males which had been released from captivity in the early part of the reintroduction period. In most cases carcasses were too decomposed to permit necropsy, but none had signs of predation. Several were apparently emaciated. The carcass of M211 was found in Otter Harbor near elephant seals (*Mirounga angustirostris*) and the carcass appeared as though it may have been crushed by elephant seals, perhaps post-mortem. Necropsy of M53 found diffuse subcutaneous hemorrhage from the shoulder to the hip on the right side, as if from a vehicle strike. Because there are no vehicles on San Miguel, and there was no evidence (such as puncture wounds) of a raptor attack, the fox likely sustained injury from a fall.

Table 1. Island fox mortalities, San Miguel Island, 2010.

PIT Tag	ID	Sex	Born	Age	Died	Mortality Cause
63E0F	M211	M	Captive	6	2/10/2010	Unknown
D1531	M205	M	Captive	6	6/1/2010	Unknown
E666D	M240	M	Captive	7	7/5/2010	Unknown
B0E36	M212	M	Captive	8	8/1/2010	Unknown
16449	M253	M	Wild	3	11/23/2010	Blunt trauma, perhaps from a fall
C2E6D	M229	M	Captive	4	12/16/2010	Unknown
03A13	F305	F	Captive	8	12/31/2010	Unknown

Wild Population Monitoring

Grid trapping in summer/fall 2010 yielded the following measures of population health:
- Density (foxes/km^2) on 4 grids
- Islandwide population estimate, extrapolated from average density
- Reproductive effort (pups/female)

Table 2. Adult density estimates for small grids, San Miguel Island, 2010.

Grid*	Date Trapped	Individ.	Density (foxes/km$^{2)}$	SE	CV**
CHAR	8/25 – 8/29	4	2.7	1.485	0.54
SAND	9/1 – 9/13	13	8.8	2.614	0.30
CARD	9/22 – 9/26	16	11.2	3.031	0.27
JACK	10/7 – 10/11	14	10.0	2.892	0.29
average			8.2	1.289	0.16

CHAR = Harris Point, CARD = Cardwell Point, SAND = Sandblast Pass, JACK = Jackass Flats
** Coefficient of Variation = standard deviation/mean

The 4 small grids were trapped from late July through late September and a total of 79 individuals (32 pups and 47 adults) were trapped. Adult density on the 4 grids ranged from 2.7–11.0 foxes/km^2, with an average density of 8.2 foxes/km^2 (Table 2). The coefficient of variation for the islandwide density estimate was 0.16 (a CV < 0.20 is desirable [M. Efford, Landcare Research, pers. comm.]). Multiplying the average density by the area of the island (38.1 km^2) yielded a population estimate of 315 adult foxes, with 80% CI = 251-378 adult foxes. When pups were included in density estimates, the islandwide population estimate was 516 foxes, with 80% CI = 437-595.

Since reintroduction began in 2004, the wild island fox population has increased (Fig. 5) due to annual reintroduction (2004-2007) and to reproduction in the wild. The annual rate of increase (λ, or lambda) was >2.0 in 2006 and 2007, and declined to <1.0 in 2008, and was 1.39 in 2009 and 1.23 in 2010 (Table 3). Average λ was 1.59 and annual values of λ have generally declined over time as the population has increased. . Values of λ >1.0 indicate an increasing population.

Table 3. Islandwide adult population estimate from grid density estimates (2006-2009) and from transect trapping (2005), San Miguel Island.

	N	SE	Variance	80% CI	lambda
2005	40*				
2006	93	18.58	345.280	70-117	2.33
2007	190	35.85	1285.50	144-235	2.04
2008	183	31.51	992.59	143-223	0.96
2009	256	37.80	1432.05	208-305	1.39
2010	315	49.77	2476.53	252-379	1.23

* Minimum number known to be alive from trapping and radiotelemetry

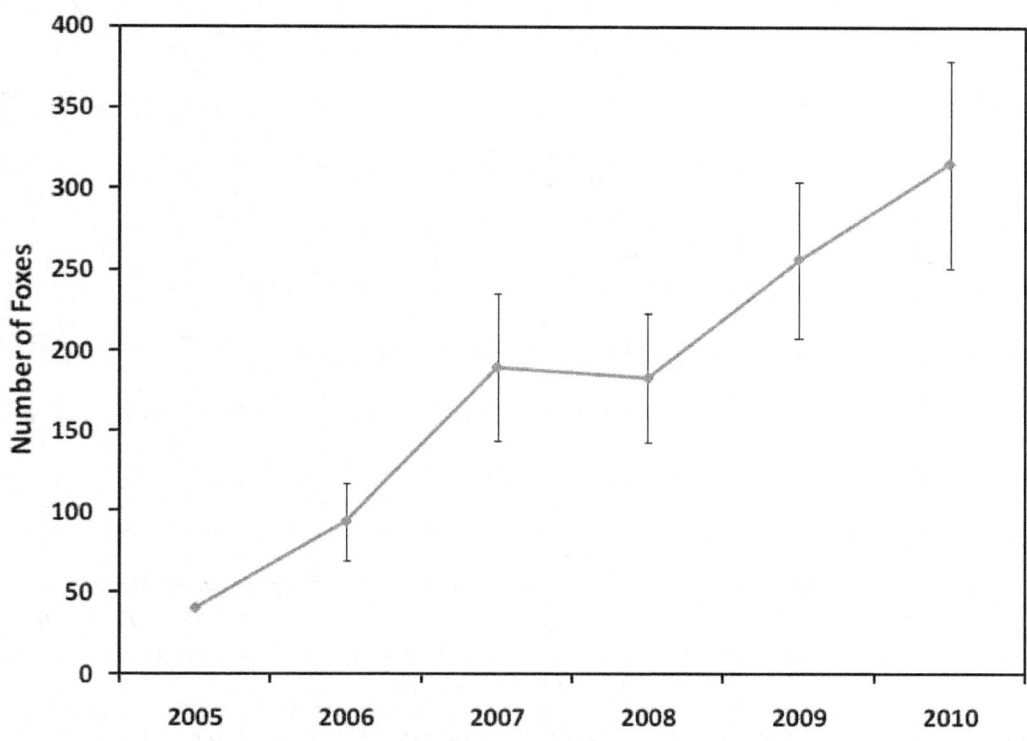

Figure 5. Islandwide adult population estimate, with 80% confidence interval, for San Miguel island foxes, from MNKA (2005) and grid-based density estimation (2006-2010).

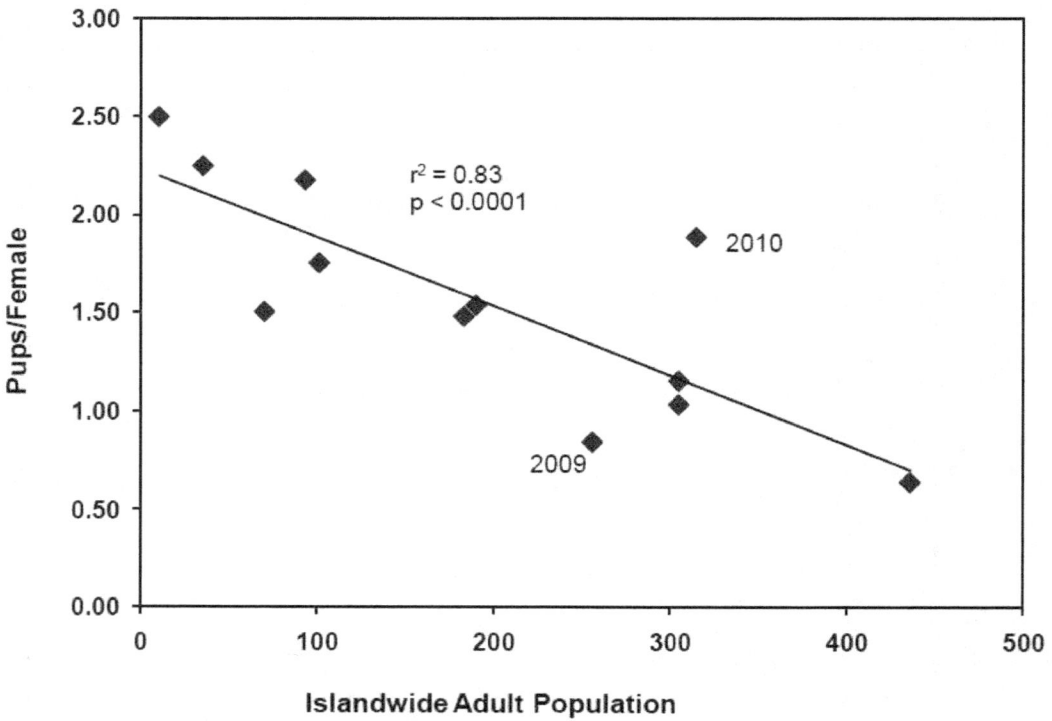

Figure 6. Regression of reproductive effort (pups/adult female) on islandwide population size, San Miguel Island, 1993-2010.

A tally of captured foxes by sex and age indicated an equal sex ratio in pups and a bias toward males in adults (Table 4). We measured reproductive success as the ratio of pups (32) to number of adult females (17) captured on the grids. The estimated reproductive success of 1.88 pups/female was relatively high, compared to the previous year's value of 0.84. When plotted with values from other years (including data from 1993-1999, encompassing the population decline), the regression of reproductive effort on adult population size showed reproductive effort declining as population increases, a density-dependent effect (Fig. 6). The 2009 value fell below the regression line, suggesting that relatively low reproduction in 2009 many be due to other factors, such as drought. The 2010 value fell above the regression line.

Table 4. Number of foxes captured, by age and sex on 4 San Miguel grids, 2010.

	Male	Female	Total
Pups	16	16	32
Adults	30	17	47
Total	46	34	79

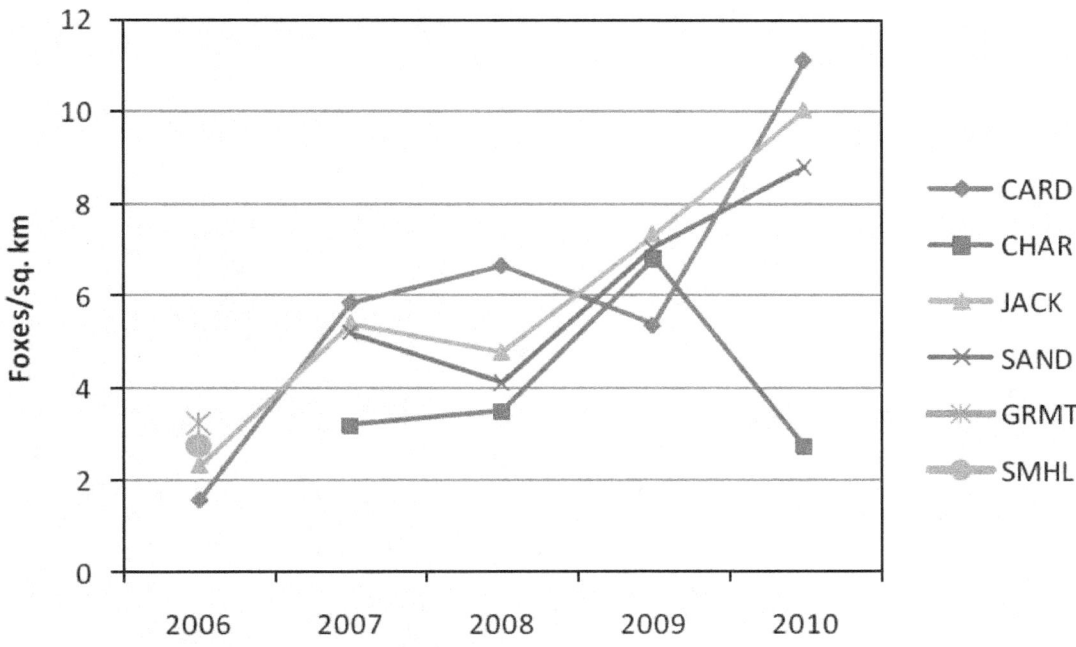

Figure 7. Adult fox density (foxes/km^2) on individual grids, San Miguel Island, 2006-2010.

Although average density and islandwide population estimate increased in 2010, on the Harris Point grid the number of foxes captured and the density declined considerably (Fig. 7). The cause of such a decline is unclear, and it may not represent a decline as much as a shift in habitat utilization. It is unlikely that a mortality cause such as predation or disease is affecting foxes on this area of the island, and not on others.

Plots of recent values of population size and mortality rate against isoclines of extinction risk continued to be encouraging. The plots of 3-year averages for 2008, 2009 and 2010 (Fig. 8) show that the 80% confidence limits for both mortality and population size fell increasingly below the 5% isocline, which is the acceptable level of risk identified in the USFWS draft island fox recovery plan. The San Miguel population reached biological recovery in 2008, and the values for 2009 and 2010 indicate even greater probability of avoiding extinction. The draft recovery plan includes other requirements for de-listing: these levels must be reached for 5 continuous years, and there must be monitoring and actions plans in place for detecting and mitigating future episodes of predation and disease. Nonetheless, the San Miguel population has retured to pre-decline levels, and can now be considered biologically recovered.

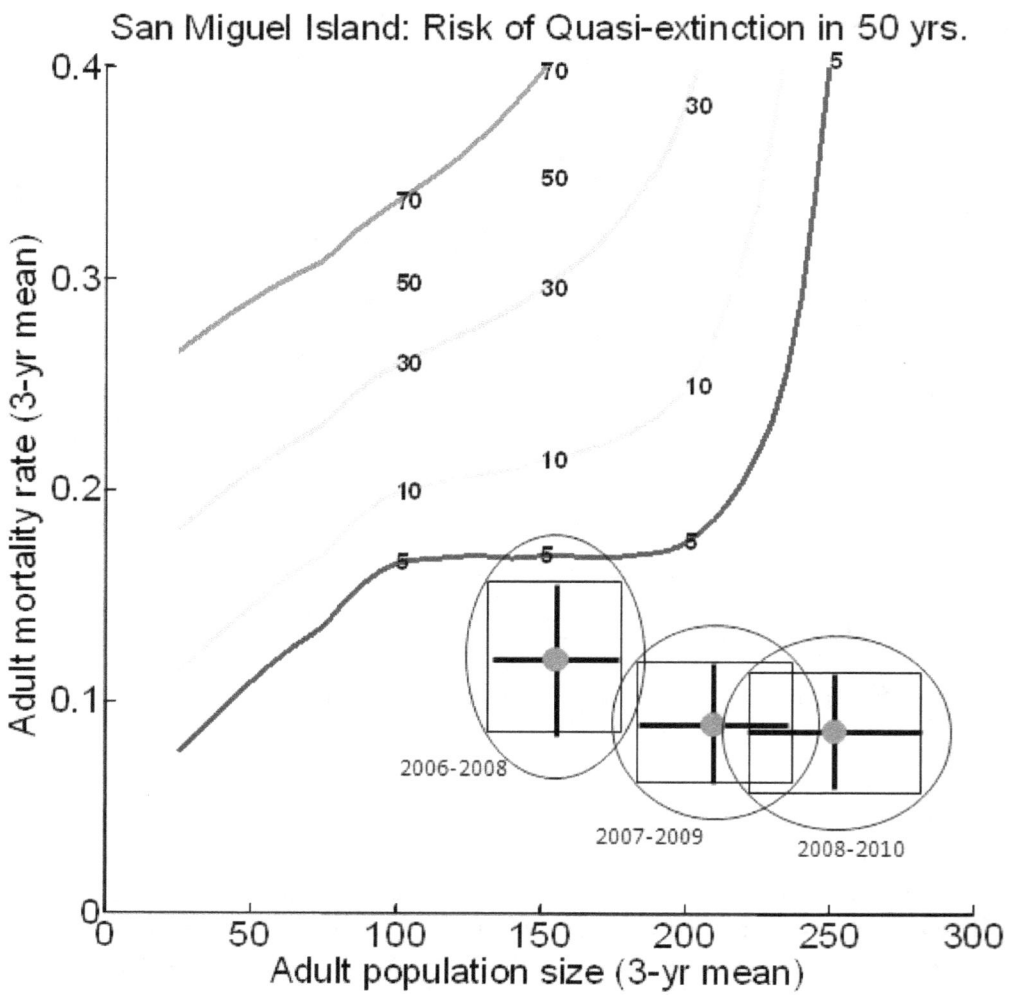

Figure 8. Extinction risk for San Miguel Island foxes under 2006-2010 averages for adult mortality and population size.

Vaccination of Wild Foxes and Establishment of Sentinel Animals

After the grids were trapped, transect trapping was conducted to manage radiocollars, establish sentinel animals for disease detection, and to vaccinate wild foxes. Between transect trapping and grid trapping, 132 foxes were captured on San Miguel in 2010. Of those foxes, 97 were vaccinated against rabies and 114 were vaccinated against CDV. On San Miguel we have been following the guidelines for small populations (< 100), that all foxes should be vaccinated for both CDV and rabies. The alternative is the "vaccinated core" strategy, in which 80-100 foxes in a certain area of the island are vaccinated against CDV (see guidelines for vaccination in Fox Health Working Group report, Schwemm 2008). This allows a portion of the population to be conferred immunity via the vaccine, and a portion to be conferred immunity via the naturally occurring strain of CDV (or other morbillivirus) that is present in all island fox populations (Clifford et al. 2006). However, in a single trapping season on San Miguel we are unlikely to trap and handle 80-100 foxes in one portion of the island (in 2010, we handled 132 islandwide). Additionally, 10-20 collared juvenile foxes should remain unvaccinated, to act as sentinel animals for detection of pathogen outbreaks. All foxes, except sentinels, will continue to be vaccinated against rabies, since there is no naturally occurring strain of rabies in island fox populations.

During the 2010 trapping season we established a sample of 14 unvaccinated, radiocollared sentinel animals (Table 5). In future years we will try to maintain a sample of at least 20 such sentinels.

Table 5. Radiocollared foxes identified as disease sentinels on San Miguel Island, 2010.

ID	PIT Tag	Sex	Age Class	Date Collared
M277	B7104	M	0	8/26/2010
M278	F5200	M	0	9/10/2010
F358	56C06	F	1	10/8/2010
F363	73E78	F	1	12/8/2010
F359	01E1A	F	1	10/8/2010
M279	D0522	M	0	9/22/2010
F357	D7D6C	F	0	9/22/2010
F355	00C50	F	1	8/26/2010
M276	07B05	M	1	8/12/2010
F360	B614D	F	2	11/11/2010
M280	52B7A	M	0	11/13/2010
F361	C2036	F	0	11/25/2010
F362	75104	F	0	11/27/2010
F356	15255	F	0	9/9/2010

Blood Samples and Serosurvey

In 2010, blood samples were collected from 117 San Miguel foxes. In 2011 a serostudy will be conducted on island fox blood samples from both San Miguel and Santa Rosa islands. Such a serostudy has not been conducted for those islands since the work by Clifford et al (2006). A total of 74 San Miguel samples will be analyzed, 19 from 2009 sampling and 55 from 2010. As per recommendations from the island fox health subgroup of the Island Fox Working Group (Appendix A in Coonan 2010), samples will be tested for antibodies to canine distermper virus (CDV), canine parvovirus (CPV), canine adenovirus (CAV) and *Toxoplasma* at Cornell University's Animal Health Diagnostic Center (Dr. Edward J. Dubovi). Samples will also be tested for antibodies to various *Leptospira* serovars at the Centers for Disease Control, Atlanta (see *Leptospira* discussion on p. 20). Results from the serostudy should be available by summer, 2011.

Future Plans

Results from monitoring in 2010 indicate that the wild population on San Miguel is still in a phase of expansion, though the annual rate of increase is decreasing. Survival is high, reproductive success is relatively high, and the average rate of increase, or lambda, from 2005 to 2010 was 1.59. With the estimated adult population >300 and total population >500, the San Miguel subspecies has finally reached what could be considered "high" population levels similar to those before the decline of the 1990s. A portion of the wild population (40-60 foxes) will be radio-collared and regularly monitored for mortality rate and causes. Trapping will be conducted in summer/fall 2011 on the 4 small grids to estimate population size and reproductive effort. A subset (80-100) of the foxes trapped in 2011 will be vaccinated against canine distemper virus to form a "vaccinated core" which would survive future outbreaks. All captured foxes will be vaccinated against rabies. In 2011 we will complete our establishment of sentinel animals. Ten to 20 juvenile (1-year old) foxes will be radiocollared but not vaccinated, in order to detect outbreaks of other types of pathogens.

Santa Rosa Island

Mortality Monitoring

Throughout 2010 we maintained a sample of 33-49 radiocollared foxes on Santa Rosa, and by the end of 2010 there were 47 radiocollared foxes on the island. Collared foxes included those released from captivity and some wild-born foxes. Annual Kaplan-Meier survival for Santa Rosa Island foxes in 2010 was 66% (80% CI = 33-49%) (Fig.4). By March 2011 the annual survival rate had climbed to 79% (80%CI = 72-86%) An annual survival rate of 80% is generally required for a stable or increasing fox population (Roemer et al. 2001). The dip in annual survival on Santa Rosa was the lowest since the heavy predation of 2005-2006.

Eleven radiocollared foxes died in 2010, 7 from predation and 2 possibly from leptospirosis (Fig. 9, Table 6). Each of those factors is discussed separately below. Given the number of predation mortalities (and we assume uncollared foxes endured a similar rate of predation mortality) and the addition of some degree of mortality due to leptospirosis, it is surprising that survival did not dip lower than it did. This may be due to the fact that the effect of both mortality factors was somewhat localized on the island. Nonetheless, the relatively poor survival in 2010 is likely the cause of the nearly 10% decline seen in the adult population this year on Santa Rosa (see Wild Population Monitoring, p. 23).

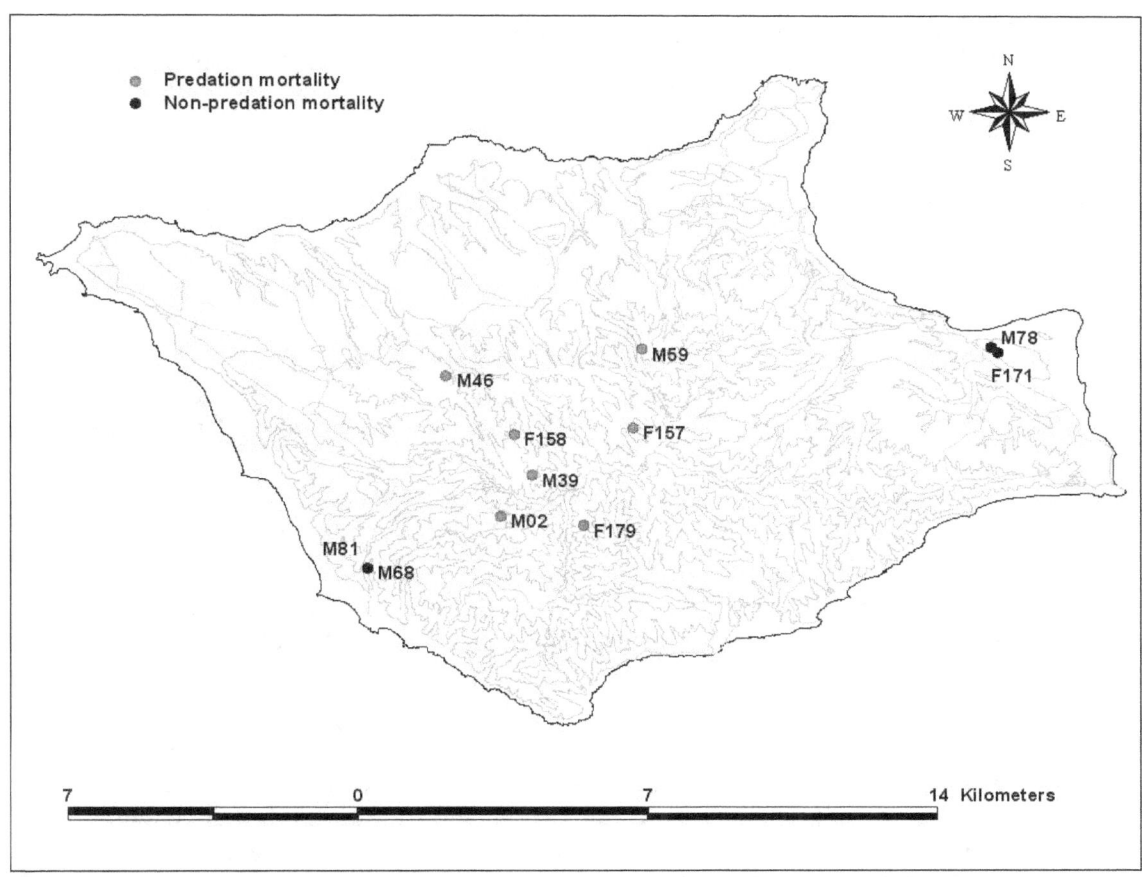

Figure 9. Location of radiocollared island fox mortalities, Santa Rosa Island, 2010.

The last fox released from the Santa Rosa captive breeding program died in 2010, due to unknown causes. M78 had been released in November 2009. Although he had had health problems in captivity, he was genetically valuable and had failed to breed in captivity. He was released in the hope that he could survive 1-2 breeding seasons and successfully breed. He was born in captivity in 2006, and found to have pneumonia during his fist vet exam, in June of that year. He was treated with antibiotics for two months. His heart was observed to be normal in June but during a September pup exam he was noted to have a grade V heart murmur audible over his entire chest and palpable on the chest wall. He was put on another course of antibiotics. The murmur remained with him throughout his life and he was given three cardiac ultrasounds in March 2007, March 2008 and November 2009 shortly before he was released. The ultrasounds showed significant heart defects, though they were likely non-congenital and caused by the pneumonia he had as a pup.

Golden Eagle Predation and Response
In February-April 2010, 7 radiocollared foxes died from eagle predation, Additionally, one radiocollared fox and one uncollared fox died from predation in November 2009.

21

Table 6. Island fox mortalities, Santa Rosa Island, 2010.

Date	PIT Tag	Other	Sex	Born	Age	Mortality Cause and Findings
2/1/2010	75125	M02	M	Captive	9	Predation
2/1/2010	65F0A	F158	F	Captive	3	Predation
2/4/2010	8024B	M78	M	Captive	4	Unknown
2/10/2010	25D54	F171	F	Captive	8	Unknown - not predation
2/14/2010	84542	F179	F	Wild	1	Predation
2/20/2010	E1D7D	M46	M	Wild	4	Predation
2/21/2010	3784A	M39	M	Captive	3	Predation
3/1/2010	D003E	F157	F	Captive	2	Predation
4/1/2010	13B68	M59	M	Captive	3	Predation
7/25/2010	E6A16	M68	M	Wild	1	Septicemia – possible leptospirosis
11/20/2010	71E45	M81	M	Wild	1	Nephritis – presumptive leptospirosis

Feathers found at one mortality site (that of M02, Fig. 9) were identified as golden eagle feathers (P. Trail, U.S. Fish and Wildlife Service, pers. comm.). On 5 March 2010 a golden eagle was observed by Institute for Wildlife Studies staff surveying for bald eagles on Santa Rosa Island, and another sighting occurred on 7 March. The initial sighting was in the Lopez Peak area, near the recent predation mortalities.

Although there are currently no predation or eagle 'triggers' which prompt a management response, NPS decided to initiate a capture attempt, due to the number of predation mortalities, the decline in annual survival, the presence of golden eagle feathers and recent credible sightings of golden eagles. In March 2010, NPS contracted with Native Range Inc. for a helicopter net-gunning golden eagle capture effort. During the survey flight on 12 March, no eagles were observed, and no further predation-caused mortalities were recorded after 1 April 2010.

Because helicopter operations failed to find and/or capture transient (non-breeding) golden eagles in both 2009 and 2010, we have developed ground-based eagle survey and capture capabilities for 2011. As part of a cooperative agreement with NPS, the Institute for Wildlife Studies has committed to conducting survey and capture efforts for golden eagles on both Santa Cruz and Santa Rosa Islands, should monitoring indicate eagle presence or predation-caused mortality.

Results of Golden Eagle Genetics Studies

Sandra Talbot of the USGS Alaska Science Center has completed the center's genetic investigations of golden eagles on the northern Channel Islands, funded by NPS, and has produced a draft report on their findings (Sonsthagen et al. 2011). The focus of the investigation was two-fold. First, biological tissue samples from golden eagles captured on the northern Channel Islands were analyzed genetically to determine affiliations with mainland eagles and to make inferences about the rate of island colonization by mainland eagles, Second, feather samples from recent predation-caused fox mortalities were analyzed to determine species (bald versus golden eagle) and number of individuals, as well as likely origin (mainland versus island).

To investigate genetic structure among island golden eagles, the Science Center extracted DNA from island and mainland golden eagle tissue samples (blood samples, feathers and egg membranes). Island samples had been collected by the Santa Cruz Predatory Bird Research Group during removal of golden eagles from the Channel Islands (Latta et al. 2005) . Microsatellite genotyping at 9 loci and mitochondrial DNA sequencing was conducted on samples from 48 island birds and 23 mainland individuals. Allelic richness was higher in the mainland population, as was heterozygosity, denoting a founder event for the island population, and subsequent genetic drift. This suggested a single or rapid colonization of the islands (a longer term colonization would have maintained similar allelic richness and heterozygosity between island mainland. Given the level of heterozygosity and the passage of only one generation on the islands, the likely founding population was 12 birds. Further, the low number of founders, the presence of only a single island haplotype and the lower number of alleles found at island loci all suggested a familial relationship among founders (the original colonization was perhaps by a family group).

Gene flow was asymmetrical between the mainland and island populations. Historical gene flow (gained from mitochondrial DNA) was from mainland to islands, whereas both long-term and short-term gene flow (gained from microsatellites) was from the islands to the mainland. Island eagles likely reached carrying capacity, due to their large territorial requirements, long life-span, and tendency to defend territories from offspring within 6 months of hatching. This likely forced young eagles from island nests to disperse to the mainland.

These results generally suggest that removal of golden eagles from the islands has and will continue to be a success, since the island colonization was a single event with less chance of re-colonization than if the original colonization had been sustained over time.

The Alaska Science Center also used molecular techniques to determine species and number of individuals from feathers found at fox carcasses in 2010. Species was determined based on sequence information from nuclear intron beta-fibrinogen, and individuals were identified based on 9 microsatellite loci. Of 11 eagle feathers associated with 2 Santa Rosa mortalities (M02 and M59; see Table 6 and Fig. 9), all were identified as being from golden eagles (earlier initial reports of one perhaps being from a bald eagle were incorrect). Microsatellite genotyping revealed 3 individuals, and none shared a genotype with any of the mainland or island birds previously sampled (thus none were eagles previously captured on the islands or mainland). The 3 individuals were identical at all but one locus, suggesting they were first-order relatives (siblings or parent-offspring), and there was high relatedness between the island individuals and a mainland bird, indicating the source of these individuals was the mainland population. Thus three related golden eagles, perhaps sub-adults, were on Santa Rosa Island in February-April 2010.

Leptospira Outbreak and Response

In 2010 there was an apparent outbreak of *Leptospira interrogans* among island foxes on Santa Rosa Island. Infection with the bacterium can result in severe renal impairment, which can lead to death (Greene and Shotts 1990). Evidence from necropsies suggests that *Leptospira* infection may have been a mortality factor for two radiocollared foxes, M68 and M81, which died in Acapulco Canyon, within 50 m of one another. M68 died in July and M81 in November 2010.

Necropsy of M81's carcass revealed lesions in the kidney, and a PCR test on kidney tissue was positive for *Leptospira* species. M68 died from bacterial septicemia. The kidneys from M68 were too autolyzed for full evaluation but the necropsy report noted glomerulopathy, thickening of the membranes of the tubules and glomeruli. Immunohistochemistry tests on tissue from M68's kidneys were positive for *Leptospira*. Thus, *Leptospira* was present in both of these carcasses, and there was kidney damage in both of them as well.

In light of these results, Dr. Winston Vickers of the Institute for Wildlife Studies advised us to test fox blood samples from that area on Santa Rosa Island for evidence of exposure to several serovars of *L. interrogans*, each of which is associated with different hosts. There are over 200 serovars of *Leptospira*, and as many as 7 have been potentially important in island foxes. We submitted blood samples from foxes in the area adjacent to the mortalities to the Animal Health Diagnostic Testing Center at Cornell University for standard microagglutination tests (MAT). Results (Table 7) indicated recent infection (titers ≥ 1600) for serovars associated with skunks and pinnipeds (Pomona) and deer mice (Bratislava), but not for the serovar associated with deer (Hardjo). Fewer foxes had titers to serovar Icterohaemorrhagiae, which is associated with rodents. Both deceased foxes had high summer titers to both Pomona and Bratislava. For three foxes we collected blood samples from both July and December. Two of those foxes showed decreasing titers, one (A2B2C) for both Pomona and Bratislava and the other (F5F25) for Bratislava. The declining titers suggested that the infection was higher in summer and was declining by December (W. Vickers, IWS, pers. comm.).

Serological testing showed that in areas further from the mortality sites, seroprevalence was less (Figs. 10 and 11). Results from an ongoing serostudy on 2009 and 2010 fox blood samples from both San Miguel and Santa Rosa Islands should determine whether the outbreak was limited to 2010, and how widely distributed the outbreak was on the island in 2010. Three 2009 Santa Rosa samples were negative for all serovars, although two of those foxes, including M68, who died in 2010, were positive in 2010. Park staff placed additional radiocollars on foxes in the China Camp area and collected additional blood samples in January –February 2011, in order to further evaluate the effect of the epidemic on Santa Rosa foxes.

Table 7. Titers at which island fox blood samples were positive for various serovars of *Leptospira interrogans*, Santa Rosa Island. Values are the maximum dilution factor (e.g., 1:800) at which samples tested positive for that serovar.

PIT Tag	Collar	Date	Sex	Age Class	Pomona (skunks, pinnipeds)	Hardjo (deer)	Icterohae-morrhagiae (rodents	Grippo-typhosa	Canicola	Bratislava (mice)	Comments
A2B2C		7/5/2010	F	1	800	<100	400	<100	<100	3200	
		12/12/2010			400	<100	400	<100	<100	1600	
C667D		7/2/2010	F	1	3200	<100	6400	<100	<100	12800	
		12/12/2010			3200	<100	3200	<100	<100	12800	
F5F25		7/1/2010	M	1	1600	<100	100	<100	<100	200	
		12/13/2010			1600	<100	<100	<100	<100	<100	
12672		8/23/2010	M	1	800	<100	400	<100	<100	3200	
2554B		12/12/2010	M	1	3200	<100	800	<100	<100	12800	
30C37		8/18/2010	M	0	<100	<100	<100	<100	<100	<100	
31439		7/11/2010	F	0	<100	<100	<100	<100	<100	<100	
32256		7/7/2010	F	0	<100	<100	<100	<100	<100	<100	
36401	M87	12/12/2010	M	0	1600	<100	200	<100	<100	400	
56141	F140	7/7/2010	F	2	200	<100	200	<100	<100	800	
62159		8/18/2010	F	0	<100	<100	<100	<100	<100	<100	
6333A		7/9/2010	M	0	<100	<100	<100	<100	<100	<100	
64939		7/16/2010	F	1	3200	<100	100	<100	<100	400	
71E45	M81	8/18/2010	M	1	1600	<100	200	<100	<100	1600	Died Nov. 2010
9283B		8/22/2010	F	1	3200	<100	400	<100	<100	1600	
96B79	F145	7/19/2010	F	2	400	<100	800	<100	<100	3200	
9741D		7/1/2010	F	1	400	<100	400	<100	<100	1600	
A6234	F178	7/19/2010	F	1	6400	<100	400	<100	<100	1600	
A7174		8/18/2010	M	1	1600	<100	200	<100	<100	1600	
C7B1B	F125	7/3/2010	F	3	400	<100	<100	<100	<100	100	
D353A	M35	7/10/2010	M	2	100	<100	100	<100	<100	400	
D700E		7/18/2010	F	0	<100	<100	<100	<100	<100	<100	
E6A16	M68	7/3/2010	M	1	1600	<100	400	<100	<100	1600	Died July 2010
E6D47		12/12/2010	F	1	1600	<100	200	<100	<100	1600	
F4F4E	F181	8/18/2010	F	0	<100	<100	<100	<100	<100	<100	Died July 2010, positive in 2010
E6A16	M68	7/22/2009	M		<100	<100	<100	<100	<100	<100	
5141C		7/22/2009	M	0	<100	<100	<100	<100	<100	<100	
C667D		7/23/2009	F	1	<100	<100	<100	<100	<100	<100	positive in 2010

Figure 10. Titers to *Leptospira interrogans* serovar Pomona in Santa Rosa island foxes, 2010. Size of the circle is proportional to dilution factor of the titer.

Figure 11. Titers to *Leptospira interrogans* serovar Bratislava in Santa Rosa island foxes, 2010. Size of the circle is proportional to dilution factor of the titer.

Table 8. Occurrence of different serovars of *Leptospira interrogans* in island foxes on different islands, as indicated by serological studies.

Island	Pomona (skunks, pinnipeds)	Hardjo (deer)	Icterohae-morrhagiae (rodents)	Grippo-typhosa	Canicola	Bratislava (mice)
San Miguel						
Santa Rosa	N, C		N			N, C
Santa Cruz			G, R			C
San Nicolas						
Santa Catalina						C
San Clemente			R			C

*N = NPS, this study; C = Clifford et al. 2006, G = Garcelon et al. 1992, R = Roemer et al. 2001

The apparent outbreak of *Leptospira* infection in an island fox population, with high titers and actual clinical symptoms of infection and impact to health, is unprecedented for island foxes. Necropsies of >500 island foxes from all islands, over a 10-year period, revealed no evidence of disease or mortalities from *Leptospira* (Munson 2010). Previous serological studies have shown island fox populations to have varying levels of non-infectious seroprevalence to various *Leptospira* serovars (Table 8; Clifford et al. 2006, Garcelon et al. 1992, Munson 2010). San Miguel and San Nicolas have never shown seroprevalence for any serovar of *Leptospira*, whereas Santa Rosa is the only island to show seroprevalence to three serovars.

It is curious why Santa Cruz Island foxes do not show evidence of exposure to serovar Pomona, since that is associated with skunks, though Bakker et al. (2006) found no evidence of exposure to Pomona in 28 skunks from Santa Cruz Island. Feral pigs were removed from Santa Cruz Island by 2006, and a serostudy of 223 pigs conducted during the removal program found antibodies to five *Leptospira* serovars, including Pomona and Bratislava (Blumenshine et al. 2009).

The serovar Pomona is also present in elephant seals in California (Colegrove et al. 2005), and it is possible that elephant seals may be the source of infection for island foxes. The area on Santa Rosa Island where high titers to Pomona (and Bratislava) occurred, as well as the two mortalities, is adjacent to an important haul-out site for elephant seals (D. Richards, NPS, pers. comm.). *Leptospira* also occurs in California sea lions (Colagrass-Schouten et al. 2002), where outbreaks of leptospirosis occur every 4-5 years, with considerable mortality (Lloyd-Smith et al. 2007). In sea lions leptospirosis is apparently endemic, and even in non-outbreak years it occurs at fairly high seroprevalence. While this would suggest that sea lions were a possible source of leptospires for Santa Rosa foxes, there are no haul-out sites for sea lions on that coast.

Leptospires can be transmitted either directly between animals, by direct contact, venereal and placental transfer, bite wounds and ingestion of infected meat, or indirectly, by contact with vegetation, soil or water which has been contaminated with *Leptospira* from an infected animal's urine (Greene and Shotts 1990). Stagnant or slow-moving water can harbor the spirochetes for a considerable time, and people are often advised to avoid contact with water near seal haul-out sites (D. Richards, NPS, pers. comm.). Thus, possible sources of contamination for foxes in the "hot zone" on Santa Rosa include prey (deer mice and, to a lesser extent, skunks), seasonal water sources in Acapulco and Trancion Canyons, and beach areas where pinnipeds haul-out.

Although the high titers to both Pomona and Bratislava suggest possible infection by as many as three hosts, those two serovars are known to cross-react at high titers, and so serological results alone are insufficient to identify the host. Consequently we are cooperating with researchers from University of California, Los Angeles, and the U.S. Department of Agriculture to identify the serovar via culture methods. In February 2011 Dr. Katherine Prager, DVM of the University of California, Davis and UCLA, obtained urine samples from 16 island foxes and spotted skunks on Santa Rosa Island. Those samples were placed in culture media and sent to Richard Zuerner of the USDA. In February 2011 *Leptospira* was successfully cultured from four of those samples (two skunk and two fox samples), and was preliminarily identified as serovar Pomona in April 2011 (R. Zuerner, USDA, pers. comm..). In fact, the particular serovar was one that had also been isolated from a stranded seal in 1970 (Zuerner and Alt 2009). Park staff will also attempt to obtain urine and blood samples from deer mice, to evaluate the possibility that deer mice serve as the host. In February 2010 Brent Stewart of the Hubbs-SeaWorld Research Institute obtained blood samples from juvenile elephant seals on San Miguel Island and at the haul-out site on Santa Rosa near where the fox mortalities and high titers occurred. Those elephant seal blood samples will be tested for antibodies to various serovars of *Leptospira*.

The two foxes for which *Leptospira* was cultured from urine are M87 and E6D47, both of which were also seropositive for *pomona* in December 2010, at 1:1600. The urine samples were taken in February, 2011, which means those foxes were actively shedding the bacteria at that time. If other infected foxes are also shedding (and 18 of 25 foxes sample were seropositive at 1:1600 or higher), island foxes themselves could be serving as the source of infection for other foxes, even if the original source was another species (J. Lloyd-Smith, University of California, Los Angeles, pers. comm.). In other words, the outbreak could be ongoing.

An appropriate management response depends upon identification of the host species, and continued monitoring for fox mortalities and antibodies to *Leptospira* in fox blood, and spirochetes (active shedding) in urine. Should further outbreak or additional *Leptospira*-associated mortalities occur, vaccination is a possible mitigation measure (W. Vickers, Institute for Wildlife Studies, pers. comm.). However, vaccine protection is serovar-specific; currently there are vaccinations for protection against serovars Icterohaemorrhagiae and Pomona, but there is no vaccine against serovar Bratislava.

Wild Population Monitoring

Trapping was conducted on the 18 ladder grids (Fig. 3) from July through early August. Targeted trapping was conducted from August 2010 through January 2011 on 27 transects in order to vaccinate foxes and replace/add radiocollars. A total of 64 foxes (49 adults and 15 pups) were trapped on grids, and density estimates for the grids ranged from 0.1 – 1.7 foxes/km^2 (Table 9). There were no foxes caught on the Johnson's Lee grid, so those trap-nights were combined with the Lighthouse Road grid for analysis. When the average density of 0.78 foxes/km^2 was applied to the island area (216 km^2), the estimated islandwide adult population was 169 foxes, with an 80% confidence interval of 128-210 and a coefficient of variation of 0.20 (Table 10). Including pups in the analysis resulted in an islandwide population estimate of 292 foxes (80% CI = 233-

351).The sex ratio was close to even for adults on the grids and transects, though there were almost twice as many male pups as female pups (Tables 11 and 12). The ratio of pups to females was low on both grids (0.63) and overall (0.78), During target trapping, 98 additional individuals were trapped, making a total of 162 foxes handled during trapping season.

Table 9. Adult density estimates for ladder grids, Santa Rosa Island, 2010.

Grid	Date Trapped	Individ.	Density (foxes/km^2)	SE	CV*
Burma Road	7/1 – 7/6	1	0.28	0.398	1.42
China Camp	7/6 – 7/10	5	1.41	0.839	0.59
Johnson' Lee/Lighthouse Road	7/7 – 7/12	1	0.14	0.200	1.43
Bee Canyon	7/7 – 7/12	2	0.56	0.510	0.92
Pocket Field	7/7 – 7/12	1	0.28	0.399	1.43
Arlington Springs	7/8 – 7/13	5	1.41	0.849	0.60
Trancion Canyon	7/14 – 7/19	3	0.84	0.626	0.75
Quemada Canyon	7/21 – 7/26	3	0.84	0.627	0.74
Wreck Canyon	7/21- 7/26	4	1.04	0.675	0.65
Old Ranch	7/21 – 7/26	2	0.56	0.514	0.91
Sierra Pablo	7/21 – 7/26	1	0.28	0.399	1.41
Signal Road	7/28 – 8/2	2	0.56	0.513	0.91
Arlington Canyon	7/28 – 8/2	3	0.85	0.626	0.74
Telephone Road	8/4 – 8/9	6	1.71	0.932	0.55
Carrington Point	8/4 – 8/9	2	0.56	0.515	0.91
Dry Canyon	8/4 – 8/9	5	1.41	0.834	0.59
Verde Canyon	8/4 – 8/9	2	0.57	0.515	0.91
average			0.78	0.149	0.19

* Coefficient of Variation = standard deviation/mean

Table 10. Islandwide density and population estimates, 2009-2010 Santa Rosa Island.

	Captures	Individuals	Avg. Density	SE	N	80% CI	CV
2009							
Adults	111	59	0.86	0.170	187	140-233	0.20
Pups Included	148	85	1.80	0.270	389	313-466	0.15
2010							
Adults	112	49	0.78	0.149	169	128-210	0.19
Pups Included	131	64	1.35	0.213	292	233-351	0.15

Table 11. Number of foxes captured, by age and sex, on 18 Santa Rosa grids, 2010.

	Male	Female	Total
Pups	10	5	15
Adults	25	24	49
Total	35	29	64

Table 12. Number of foxes captured, by age and sex, on 18 Santa Rosa grids and 27 transects, 2010.

	Male	Female	Total
Pups	29	18	47
Adults	55	60	115
Total	84	78	162

Between 2009 and 2010 the island fox population on Santa Rosa declined, and the drop was reflected in population estimates from adults (10% decline) and adults and pups combined (25% decline). Island fox survival on Santa Rosa dipped to below 70% in 2010 (Fig. 4), and was as low as 60% in mid-2010. The low survival could explain the population decline in adults, and the low reproductive rate (pups/female) likely contributed to the 25% decline in the overall population. Certainly the predation in winter-spring 2009-2010 contributed to reduced survival and the observed population decline. The two *Leptospira*-associated mortalities occurred in July and November 2010, during and after annual grid trapping for density estimation. The effect of such disease-influenced mortality may not be reflected in the 2010 estimates of density and islandwide population.

On the other hand, the area of the island where the *Leptospira* mortalities and high seroprevalence occurred saw the biggest drop in density (Fig. 12). Density fell by over 80% in the Johnson's Lee/Lighthouse Road area. Several other large declines occurred adjacent to the area of predation mortalities. Predation was somewhat a local phenomenon, and islandwide serological testing will reveal whether *Leptospira* is a local issue or whether foxes and/or other hosts are spreading it islandwide. Since November 2010 there has been one mortality of a radiocollared fox. It died in February 2011 in upper Arlington Canyon, at considerable distance from the "hot zone". Its carcass was too decayed to evaluate condition of kidneys or presence of *Leptospira* in tissues.

To determine whether the Santa Rosa population was approaching biological recovery, we plotted 3-year averages of adult population size and adult mortality using the spreadsheet tool developed by Vicki Bakker of the University of Arizona, as we did for San Miguel. The plots of 3-year averages for 2008, 2009 and 2010 (Fig. 13) show that the Santa Rosa subspecies, in contrast to the three other listed subspecies, still has a relatively high probability of extinction in the near to mid-term. This is due to the lower annual survival and lower population size in 2010, and underscores the importance of mounting an effective response to future predation-caused mortalities. There has been no predation-caused mortality on Santa Rosa in winter-spring 2010/2011, and the park now has ground-based eagle survey and capture capability, via an agreement with IWS. Survival increased in early 2011 (see Fig. 4) and we may expect higher fox densities in 2011.

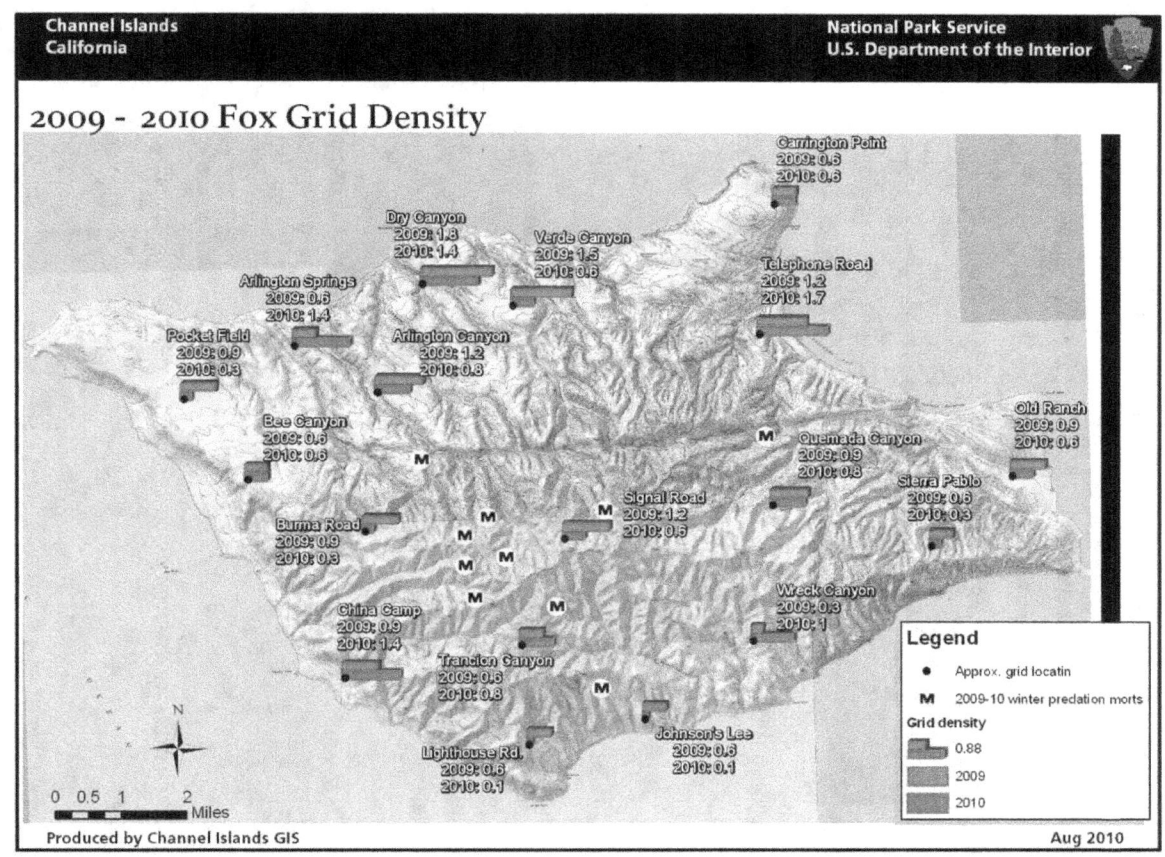

Figure 12. Comparison of 2009 and 2010 densities at 18 trapping grids, Santa Rosa Island.

Density of Island Spotted Skunks

We have marked individual skunks with PIT tags since 2006. Since 2009, when we began grid trapping, we have been able to estimate density of skunks on the island using program Density and the grid trapping data. The resulting estimates are for all skunks, since adults could not be distinguished from juveniles. The number of individual skunks, and thus the density, varied on the 18 ladder grids (Table 13). No skunks were trapped on the Sierra Pablo grid or the Verde Canyon grid. Applying the average density of 13.5 skunks/km^2 to the island's area (216 km^2) resulted in an islandwide density estimate of 2,911 skunks, with an 80% confidence interval of 2,373 – 3,733 and coefficient of variation of 0.14. With an islandwide estimate of 389 foxes, skunks were almost 8 times as abundant as foxes.

33

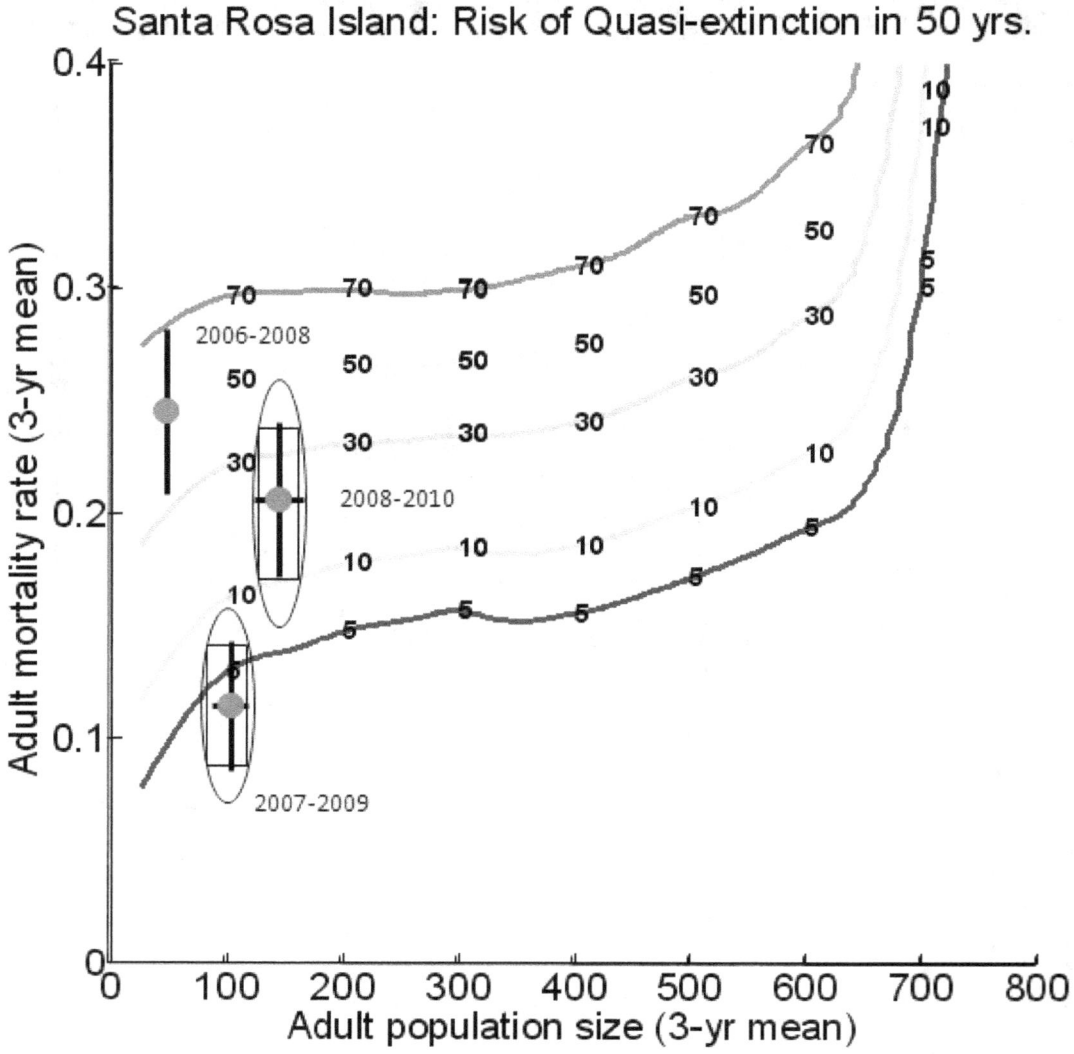

Figure 13. Extinction risk for Santa Rosa Island foxes under 2006-2010 averages for adult mortality and population size.

Far fewer skunks were caught on the monitoring grids in 2010 (71 individuals) than in 2009 (132). However, the estimated density and islandwide population was similar to that in 2009, when the population estimate was 3,013 (80%CI = 2,652 – 3,376). Program Density may have overestimated the 2010 density of skunks, perhaps due to the relatively low number of recaptures. Of the 71 skunks caught on grids in 2010, 58, or 82%, were caught only once. In 2009, 67% of the 132 skunks were caught once, and there was a higher proportion of recaptures.

Table 13. Density of island spotted skunks on ladder grids, Santa Rosa Island, 2010.

Grid	Date Trapped	Individ.	Density (skunks/km^2)	SE	CV*
Burma Road	7/1 – 7/6	1	3.6	4.853	1.35
China Camp	7/6 – 7/10	3	10.8	7.325	0.68
Lighthouse Road	7/7 – 7/12	7	12.5	5.694	0.45
Johnson's Lee	7/7 – 7/12	3	10.7	7.284	0.68
Bee Canyon	7/7 – 7/12	1	3.6	4.865	1.35
Pocket Field	7/7 – 7/12	2	7.1	6.085	0.85
Arlington Springs	7/8 – 7/13	4	14.4	8.462	0.59
Trancion Canyon	7/14 – 7/19	5	18.0	9.484	0.53
Quemada Canyon	7/21 – 7/26	7	25.2	11.421	0.45
Wreck Canyon	7/21- 7/26	6	21.5	10.481	0.49
Old Ranch	7/21 – 7/26	2	7.3	6.143	0.85
Sierra Pablo	7/21 – 7/26	0	0.0		
Signal Road	7/28 – 8/2	4	14.6	8.515	0.58
Arlington Canyon	7/28 – 8/2	5	18.0	9.523	0.53
Telephone Road	8/4 – 8/9	6	21.4	10.404	0.49
Carrington Point	8/4 – 8/9	10	35.7	14.131	0.40
Dry Canyon	8/4 – 8/9	5	18.1	9.484	0.53
Verde Canyon	8/4 – 8/9	0	0.0		
average			13.5		

* Coefficient of Variation = standard deviation/mean

The relative number of foxes and skunks trapped during annual monitoring suggests that skunks, although still very abundant, are starting to decline as the Santa Rosa fox population recovers (Figure 14). Both the number of total captures and the number of total individuals indicates that since 2006 the relative abundance of foxes has increased, whereas that of skunks has decreased. Given the 2009 skunk population estimate of 3,014 and the apparent decline in skunks, the skunk population in previous years may have been as high as 4,000.

a)

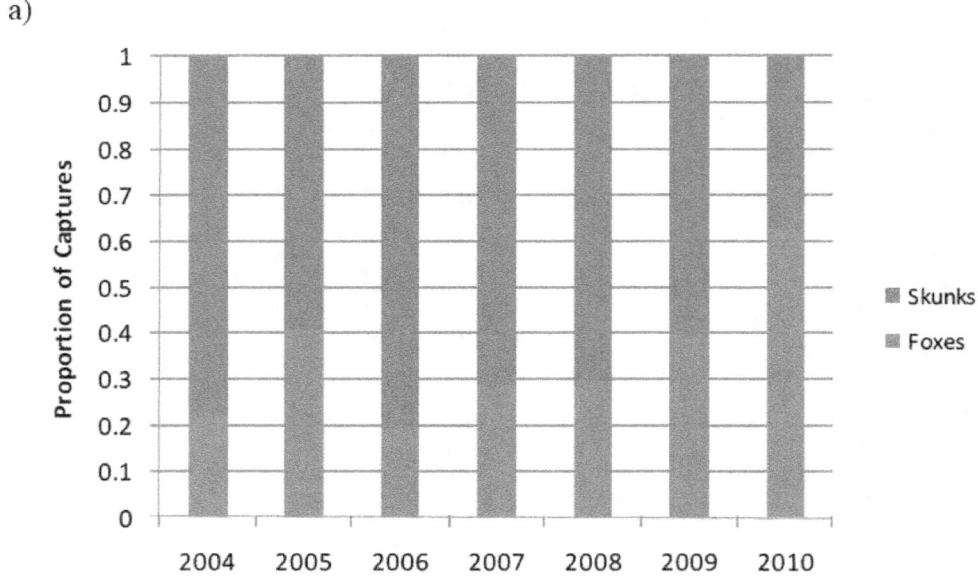

b)

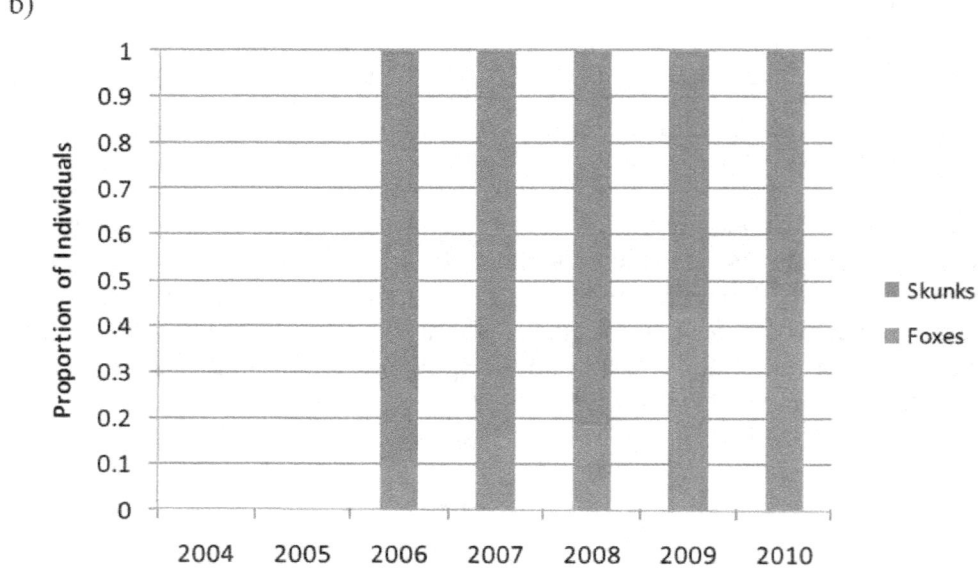

Figure 14 . Proportion of captures (a) and individuals (b) for island foxes and island spotted skunks trapped during annual population monitoring on Santa Rosa Island, 2004-2010.

Vaccination of Wild Foxes and Establishment of Sentinel Animals

After the grids were trapped, transect trapping was conducted to manage radiocollars, establish sentinel animals for disease detection, and to vaccinate wild foxes. Of the 162 foxes caught on girds and transects, 111 were vaccinated against rabies and 114 were vaccinated against distemper. We would have vaccinated all foxes against rabies, but we did not have enough vaccinations on hand. Thirteen foxes received an initial distemper vaccination as well as a booster, because they had not been vaccinated prior to 2010 and were caught at least twice. As on San Miguel, we have been following the guidelines for small populations (< 100), that all foxes should be vaccinated for both CDV and rabies. The alternative is the 'vaccinated core' strategy, in which 80-100 foxes in a certain area of the island are vaccinated against CDV (see guidelines for vaccination in Fox Health Working Group report, Appendix A in Coonan 2010). This allows a portion of the population to be conferred immunity via the vaccine, and a portion to be conferred immunity via the naturally occurring strain of CDV (or other morbillivirus) that is present in all island fox populations (Clifford et al. 2006). Recommendations from the health group of the Island Fox working Group are to switch to the vaccinated core strategy when a population reaches about 50% of the recovery goal. With less than 200 adults in the Santa Rosa population, we are not yet at 50% of the recovery goal. We also have a goal of leaving 10-20 collared juvenile foxes unvaccinated, to act as sentinel animals for detection of pathogen outbreaks. All foxes, except sentinels, will continue to be vaccinated against rabies, since there is no naturally occurring strain of rabies in island fox populations.

During the 2010 trapping season we established a sample of 15 unvaccinated, radiocollared sentinel animals (Table 14). In future years we will try to maintain a sample of at least 20 such sentinels.

Table 14. Radiocollared foxes identified as disease sentinels on Santa Rosa Island, 2010.

ID	PIT Tag	Sex	Age Class	Date Collared
M87	36401	M	0	12/12/2010
F186	F1155	F	0	11/15/2010
M86	25401	M	0	10/4/2010
M85	C6561	M	0	10/3/2010
F185	05678	F	0	10/2/2010
M84	21E0F	M	0	10/2/2010
F184	12843	F	1	9/30/2010
M83	A5825	M	1	9/30/2010
F183	B2D60	F	1	8/21/2010
M82	95C6F	M	0	8/23/2010
F182	F0B62	F	0	8/18/2010
F181	F4F4E	F	0	8/18/2010
M81	71E45	M	1	8/18/2010
M80	A3039	M	1	7/12/2010
M79	B0712	M	1	7/8/2010

Blood Samples and Serosurvey

In 2010, blood samples were collected from 139 Santa Rosa foxes. In 2011 a serostudy will be conducted on island fox blood samples form both San Miguel and Santa Rosa islands. Such a serostudy has not been conducted for those islands since the work by Clifford et al (2006). A total of 70 Santa Rosa samples will be analyzed, 40 from 2009 sampling and 30 from 2010. As per recommendations from the island fox health subgroup of the Island Fox Working Group

(Appendix A in Coonan 2010), samples will be tested for antibodies to canine distermper virus (CDV), canine parvovirus (CPV), canine adenovirus (CAV) and *Toxoplasma* at Cornell University's Animal Health Diagnostic Center (Dr. Edward J. Dubovi). Samples will also be tested for antibodies to 20 *Leptospira* serovars at the Centers for Disease Control, Atlanta. Results from the serostudy should be available by late spring, 2011.

Future Plans

Conducting trapping on ladder grids in 2009 and 2010 has allowed estimation of Santa Rosa Island fox density and population size. In 2009 adult population size was estimated to be 187, with an overall population estimate of 389 when pups were included, and wild reproduction remained relatively high. Those population levels were in the range of those required for recovery, provided adult survival remained high (Bakker and Doak 2009). However, Santa Rosa Island fox population size and survival declined in 2010 due to eagle predation, and there is the possibility that a disease caused by bacteria (*Leptospira*) may be another mortality factor for this population. Mortality monitoring and grid monitoring with density/population estimation in 2011 will indicate whether these mortality factors remain prevalent in 2011, and whether the previous trajectory of population recovery is reestablished.

In 2011 we will continue to implement recovery actions for island foxes on Santa Rosa Island. We will maintain a sample of >50 radiocollared foxes on the island. We will conduct population monitoring in summer/fall 2011, using small ladder grids (Rubin et al. 2006). All newly encountered wild animals will be PIT-tagged, and all captured foxes will be vaccinated against canine distemper virus and rabies, and blood samples will be drawn from a susbset of the island foxes we trap. Additionally, we will conduct a serosurvey on previously collected blood samples to determine fox exposure to various diseases, including exposure to various serovars of *Leptospira*. We will also attempt to culture *Leptospira* from island fox and skunk urine samples.

Literature Cited

Bakker, V.J. and D.F. Doak. 2009. Population viability management: ecological standards to guide adaptive management for rare species. Frontiers in Ecology and the Environment 7:158-165.

Bakker, V.J., D.F. Doak, G.W. Roemer, D.K. Garcelon, T.J. Coonan, S.A. Morrison, C. Lynch, K. Ralls, and R. Shaw. 2009. Incorporating ecological drivers and uncertainty into a demographic viability analysis for the island fox. Ecological Monographs 79(1):77-108.

Bakker, V.,D. Van Vuren, K. Crooks, C. Scott, J. Wilcox and D. Garcelon. 2006. Serologic survey of the island spotted skunk on Santa Cruz Island. Western North American Naturalist 66:8-12.

Blumenshine, K.M., H. Kinde and S. Patton. 2009. Biometric and disease surveillance of an insular population of feral pigs on Santa Cruz Island, California. Pgs. 387-402 *in* Damiani, C.C. and D.K. Garcelon, eds., Proceedings of the Seventh California Islands Symposium, Oxnard, California, February 5-8, 2008. Institute for Wildlife Studies, Arcata, California.

Clifford, D. L., J. A. K. Mazet, E. J. Dubovi, D. K. Garcelon, T. J. Coonan, P. A. Conrad and L. Munson. 2006. Pathogen exposure in endangered island fox (*Urocyon littoralis*) populations: Implications for conservation management. Biological Conservation 131:230-243.

Colagross-Schouten A.M., J.A. Mazet , F.M. Gulland, M.A. Miller and S. Hietala. 2002. Diagnosis and seroprevalence of leptospirosis in California sea lions from coastal California. Journal of Wildlife Diseases 38(1):7-17.

Colegrov, K.M., L.J. Lowenstine and F.M. Gulland. 2005. Leptospirosis in northern elephant seals (*Mirounga angustirostris*) stranded along the California coast. Journal of Wildlife Diseases 41(2):426-430.

Collins, P.W. 1993. Taxonomic and biogeographic relationships of the island fox (*Urocyon littoralis*) and gray fox (*U. cinereoargenteus*) from western North America. Pp. 351-390 in Hochberg, F.G., ed., Third California Islands Symposium: Recent Advances in Research on the California Islands. Santa Barbara Museum of Natural History, Santa Barbara, CA. Proceedings of the Third California Islands Symposium.

Collins, P.W. and B.C. Latta. 2006. Nesting season diet of golden eagles on Santa Cruz and Santa Rosa Islands, Santa Barbara County, California. Santa Barbara Museum of Natural History Technical Reports – No. 3.

Cooch, E, and G. White. 2006. Program MARK: a gentle introduction. 5th edition. Available online at http://www.phidot.org/software/mark/docs/book/.

Coonan, T. J. 2003. Recovery strategy for island foxes (*Urocyon littoralis*) on the northern Channel Islands. National Park Service, Channel Islands National Park, Ventura, CA. 81 pp.

Coonan, T.J. 2010. Twelfth annual meeting, island fox working group, summary report. unpublished report on file at headquarters, Channel Islands National Park.

Coonan, T.J. 2011. 2010 annual report for island fox recovery actions conducted under permit TE086267-0 by the National Park Service, Channel Islands National Park. Unpublished report submitted to Ventura Fish and Wildlife Office, April 1, 2011. 34 pp.

Coonan, T.J., G. Austin, and C. Schwemm. 1998. Status and trend of island fox, San Miguel Island, Channel Islands National Park. Technical Report 98-01, National Park Service, Ventura, California. 27 pp.

Coonan, T. J., K. McCurdy, K. A. Rutz, M. Dennis, S. Provinsky and S. Coppelli. 2005a. Island fox recovery program 2004 annual report. Technical Report 05-07. National Park Service. 63 pp.

Coonan, T.J. and K. Rutz. 2001. Island fox captive breeding program 1999-2000 annual report. Technical Report 01-01. National Park Service, Ventura, California. 38 pp.

Coonan, T.J., K. A. Rutz, K. McCurdy, D.K. Garcelon, B.C. Latta and L. Munson. 2004. Island fox recovery program, 2003 annual report. Technical Report 04-02. National Park Service, Ventura, California. 65 pp.

Coonan, T.J. and C.A. Schwemm. 2009. Factors contributing to success of island fox reintroductions on San Miguel and Santa Rosa Islands, California. Pp. 363-376 in, Damiani, C.C and D.K. Garcelon, eds., Proceedings of the Seventh California Islands Symposium, Oxnard, California, February 5-8, 2008. Institute for Wildlife Studies, Arcata, California.

Coonan, T.J., C.A. Schwemm and D.K. Garcelon. 2010. Decline and recovery of the island fox: a case history for population recovery. Cambridge University Press, UK. 212 pp.

Coonan, T.J., C.A. Schwemm, G.W. Roemer, D.K. Garcelon, and L. Munson. 2005b. Decline of an island fox subspecies to near extinction. Southwestern Naturalist 50(1):32-41.

Davis, G. E., K. R. Faulkner, and W. L. Halvorson. 1994. Ecological Monitoring in Channel Islands National Park, California. The Fourth California Islands Symposium: update on the Status of Resources. W. L. Halvorson and G. J. Maender, editors. Santa Barbara Museum of Natural History, Santa Barbara, CA.

Efford, M. G., D. K. Dawson, and C. S. Robbins. 2004. DENSITY: software for analyzing capture-recapture data from passive detector arrays. Animal Biodiversity and Conservation 27 (1):217-228.

Fellers, G.M., C.A. Drost and B.W. Arnold. 1988. Terrestrial vertebrates monitoring handbook. Unpublished report on file at park headquarters, Channel Islands National Park, Ventura, CA.

Garcelon, D. K., R. K. Wayne and B. J. Gonzales. 1992. A serologic survey of the island fox (*Urocyon littoralis*) on the Channel Islands, California. Journal of Wildlife Diseases 28:223-229.

Greene, C.E. and E.B. Shotts. 1990. Leptosirosis. Pages 498-507 in Greene, C.E, ed., Infectious diseases of the dog and cat. W.B. Saunders, Philadelphia, Pennsylvania.

Latta, B.C., D. D. Driscoll, J. L. Linthicum, R. E. Jackman and G. Doney. 2005. Capture and translocation of golden eagles from the California Channel Islands to mitigate depredation of endemic island foxes. Pp. 341-350 in, Garcelon, D.K. and C. A. Schwemm, eds., Proceedings of the Sixth California Islands Symposium. National Park Service Technical Publication CHIS-05-01, Institute for Wildlife Studies, Arcata, California.

Lloyd-Smith, J.O., D.J. Greig, S. Hietala, G.S. Ghneim, L. Palmer, J. St, Leger, B.T. Grenfell, and F.M.D. Gulland. 2007. Cyclical changes in seroprevalence of leptospirosis in California sea lions: endemic and epidemic disease in one host species? BMC Infectious Diseases 7: 125.

Munson, L. 2010. Chapter 11: Disease of island foxes. Pages 129-143 in Coonan, T.J., C.A Schwemm and D.K. Garcelon, Decline and Recovery of the Island Fox: a Case Study for Population Recovery. Cambridge University Press, Cambridge, UK.

Pollock, K. H., S. R. Winterstein and M. J. Conroy. 1989. Estimation and analysis of survival distributions for radio-tagged animals. Biometrics 45:99–109.

Roemer, G.W. 1999. The ecology and conservation of the island fox (*Urocyon littoralis*). Ph. D. dissertation, University of California, Los Angeles, California. 229 pp.

Roemer, G.W., T.J. Coonan, D.K. Garcelon, J. Bascompte, and L. Laughrin. 2001. Feral pigs facilitate hyperpredation by golden eagles and indirectly cause the decline of the island fox. Animal Conservation 4:307-318.

Roemer, G.W., D.K. Garcelon, T.J. Coonan, and C. Schwemm. 1994. The use of capture-recapture methods for estimating, monitoring, and conserving island fox populations. Pp. 387-400 in Halvorson, W.L. and G.J. Maender, eds. The Fourth California Channel Islands Symposium: Update on the Status of Resources. Santa Barbara Museum of Natural History, Santa Barbara, CA.

Rubin, E. S., V. J. Bakker, M. G. Efford, B. S. Cohen, J. A. Stallcup, W. D. Spencer and S. A. Morrison. 2007. A population monitoring framework for five subspecies of island fox (*Urocyon littoralis*). Prepared by the Conservation Biology Institute and The Nature Conservancy for the Recovery Coordination Group of the Island Fox Integrated Recovery Team. U.S. Fish and Wildlife Service, Ventura, California.

Schwemm, C. 2008. Tenth annual meeting, island fox working group; summary report. Unpublished report on file at headquarters, Channel Islands National Park.

Timm, S.F., L. Munson, B.A. Summers, K.A. Terio, E.J. Dubovi, C.E. Rupprecht, S. Kapil and D.K. Garcelon. 2009. A suspected canine distemper epidemic as the cause of a catastrophic decline in Santa Catalina Island foxes (*Urocyon littoralis catalinae*).Journal of Wildlife Diseases 45:333-343.

U.S. Fish and Wildlife Service. 2004. Listing of the San Miguel island fox, Santa Rosa island Fox, Santa Cruz island fox, and Santa Catalina island fox as endangered; final rule. Federal Register 69(44):10335-10353.

Wayne, R.K., S.B. George, D. Gilbert, P.W. Collins, S.D. Girman and N. Lehman. 1991. A morphologic and genetic study of the island fox, Urocyon littoralis. Evolution 45:1849-1868.

Zuerner, R.L. and D.P. alt. 2009. Variable nucleotide tandem-repeat analysis revealing a unique group of *Leptospira interrogans* serovar Pomona isolates associated with California sea lions. Journal of Clinical Microbiology 47(4):1202-1205.

NPS 159/105491, August 2010